AF730451

Personal Details

Name ______________________________

Address ______________________________

____

Email Address ______________________________

Phone # ______________________________

Notary Log Book Details

Log Book # ________

Log Start Date ________

Log Finish Date ________

NOTARY RECORD

Printed Name and Address of Signer:	Phone Number:	Thumb Print:
	Email:	
	Signer's Signature:	

Service Performed:	Identification:		I.D. Number:	
☐ Oath	☐ I.D Card	☐ Credible Witness	Issued By:	
☐ Acknowledgment	☐ Drivers License	☐ Known Personally	Issued Date:	Expiration Date:
☐ Jurat	☐ Passport			
☐ Other:	☐ Other:			
Document Type:	Date/Time Notarized: AM PM		Document Date:	Fee Charged:

Printed Name and Address of Witness:	Witness' Signature:
1.	1.
2.	2.

Comments :	Record Number:

NOTARY RECORD

Printed Name and Address of Signer:	Phone Number:	Thumb Print:
	Email:	
	Signer's Signature:	

Service Performed:	Identification:		I.D. Number:	
☐ Oath	☐ I.D Card	☐ Credible Witness	Issued By:	
☐ Acknowledgment	☐ Drivers License	☐ Known Personally	Issued Date:	Expiration Date:
☐ Jurat	☐ Passport			
☐ Other:	☐ Other:			
Document Type:	Date/Time Notarized: AM PM		Document Date:	Fee Charged:

Printed Name and Address of Witness:	Witness' Signature:
1.	1.
2.	2

Comments :	Record Number:

NOTARY RECORD

Printed Name and Address of Signer:	Phone Number:	Thumb Print:
	Email:	
	Signer's Signature:	

Service Performed:
- ☐ Oath
- ☐ Acknowledgment
- ☐ Jurat
- ☐ Other:

Identification:
- ☐ I.D Card
- ☐ Credible Witness
- ☐ Drivers License
- ☐ Known Personally
- ☐ Passport
- ☐ Other:

I.D. Number:	
Issued By:	
Issued Date:	Expiration Date:

Document Type:	Date/Time Notarized: AM PM	Document Date:	Fee Charged:

Printed Name and Address of Witness:	Witness' Signature:
1.	1.
2.	2.

Comments :	Record Number:

NOTARY RECORD

Printed Name and Address of Signer:	Phone Number:	Thumb Print:
	Email:	
	Signer's Signature:	

Service Performed:
- ☐ Oath
- ☐ Acknowledgment
- ☐ Jurat
- ☐ Other:

Identification:
- ☐ I.D Card
- ☐ Credible Witness
- ☐ Drivers License
- ☐ Known Personally
- ☐ Passport
- ☐ Other:

I.D. Number:	
Issued By:	
Issued Date:	Expiration Date:

Document Type:	Date/Time Notarized: AM PM	Document Date:	Fee Charged:

Printed Name and Address of Witness:	Witness' Signature:
1.	1.
2.	2

Comments :	Record Number:

NOTARY RECORD

Printed Name and Address of Signer:	**Phone Number:**	**Thumb Print:**
	Email:	
	Signer's Signature:	

Service Performed: ☐ Oath ☐ Acknowledgment ☐ Jurat ☐ Other:	**Identification:** ☐ I.D Card ☐ Credible Witness ☐ Drivers License ☐ Known Personally ☐ Passport ☐ Other:	**I.D. Number:**	
		Issued By:	
		Issued Date:	**Expiration Date:**
Document Type:	**Date/Time Notarized:** AM PM	**Document Date:**	**Fee Charged:**

Printed Name and Address of Witness: **1.** **2.**	**Witness' Signature:** **1.** **2.**
Comments :	**Record Number:**

NOTARY RECORD

Printed Name and Address of Signer:	**Phone Number:**	**Thumb Print:**
	Email:	
	Signer's Signature:	

Service Performed: ☐ Oath ☐ Acknowledgment ☐ Jurat ☐ Other:	**Identification:** ☐ I.D Card ☐ Credible Witness ☐ Drivers License ☐ Known Personally ☐ Passport ☐ Other:	**I.D. Number:**	
		Issued By:	
		Issued Date:	**Expiration Date:**
Document Type:	**Date/Time Notarized:** AM PM	**Document Date:**	**Fee Charged:**

Printed Name and Address of Witness: **1.** **2.**	**Witness' Signature:** **1.** **2**
Comments :	**Record Number:**

NOTARY RECORD

Printed Name and Address of Signer:	**Phone Number:**	**Thumb Print:**
	Email:	
	Signer's Signature:	

Service Performed: ☐ Oath ☐ Acknowledgment ☐ Jurat ☐ Other:	**Identification:** ☐ I.D Card ☐ Credible Witness ☐ Drivers License ☐ Known Personally ☐ Passport ☐ Other:	**I.D. Number:**	
		Issued By:	
		Issued Date:	**Expiration Date:**
Document Type:	**Date/Time Notarized:** AM PM	**Document Date:**	**Fee Charged:**

Printed Name and Address of Witness: **1.** **2.**	**Witness' Signature:** **1.** **2.**
Comments :	**Record Number:**

NOTARY RECORD

Printed Name and Address of Signer:	**Phone Number:**	**Thumb Print:**
	Email:	
	Signer's Signature:	

Service Performed: ☐ Oath ☐ Acknowledgment ☐ Jurat ☐ Other:	**Identification:** ☐ I.D Card ☐ Credible Witness ☐ Drivers License ☐ Known Personally ☐ Passport ☐ Other:	**I.D. Number:**	
		Issued By:	
		Issued Date:	**Expiration Date:**
Document Type:	**Date/Time Notarized:** AM PM	**Document Date:**	**Fee Charged:**

Printed Name and Address of Witness: **1.** **2.**	**Witness' Signature:** **1.** **2**
Comments :	**Record Number:**

NOTARY RECORD

Printed Name and Address of Signer:	Phone Number:	Thumb Print:
	Email:	
	Signer's Signature:	

Service Performed:	Identification:		I.D. Number:	
☐ Oath	☐ I.D Card	☐ Credible Witness	Issued By:	
☐ Acknowledgment	☐ Drivers License	☐ Known Personally		
☐ Jurat	☐ Passport		Issued Date:	Expiration Date:
☐ Other:	☐ Other:			
Document Type:	Date/Time Notarized: AM PM		Document Date:	Fee Charged:

Printed Name and Address of Witness:	Witness' Signature:
1.	1.
2.	2.

Comments :	Record Number:

NOTARY RECORD

Printed Name and Address of Signer:	Phone Number:	Thumb Print:
	Email:	
	Signer's Signature:	

Service Performed:	Identification:		I.D. Number:	
☐ Oath	☐ I.D Card	☐ Credible Witness	Issued By:	
☐ Acknowledgment	☐ Drivers License	☐ Known Personally		
☐ Jurat	☐ Passport		Issued Date:	Expiration Date:
☐ Other:	☐ Other:			
Document Type:	Date/Time Notarized: AM PM		Document Date:	Fee Charged:

Printed Name and Address of Witness:	Witness' Signature:
1.	1.
2.	2

Comments :	Record Number:

NOTARY RECORD

Printed Name and Address of Signer:	**Phone Number:**	**Thumb Print:**
	Email:	
	Signer's Signature:	

Service Performed: ☐ Oath ☐ Acknowledgment ☐ Jurat ☐ Other:	**Identification:** ☐ I.D Card ☐ Credible Witness ☐ Drivers License ☐ Known Personally ☐ Passport ☐ Other:	**I.D. Number:**	
		Issued By:	
		Issued Date:	**Expiration Date:**
Document Type:	**Date/Time Notarized:** AM PM	**Document Date:**	**Fee Charged:**

Printed Name and Address of Witness: **1.** **2.**	**Witness' Signature:** **1.** **2.**
Comments :	**Record Number:**

NOTARY RECORD

Printed Name and Address of Signer:	**Phone Number:**	**Thumb Print:**
	Email:	
	Signer's Signature:	

Service Performed: ☐ Oath ☐ Acknowledgment ☐ Jurat ☐ Other:	**Identification:** ☐ I.D Card ☐ Credible Witness ☐ Drivers License ☐ Known Personally ☐ Passport ☐ Other:	**I.D. Number:**	
		Issued By:	
		Issued Date:	**Expiration Date:**
Document Type:	**Date/Time Notarized:** AM PM	**Document Date:**	**Fee Charged:**

Printed Name and Address of Witness: **1.** **2.**	**Witness' Signature:** **1.** **2**
Comments :	**Record Number:**

NOTARY RECORD

Printed Name and Address of Signer:	Phone Number:	Thumb Print:
	Email:	
	Signer's Signature:	

Service Performed:	Identification:		I.D. Number:	
☐ Oath	☐ I.D Card	☐ Credible Witness	Issued By:	
☐ Acknowledgment	☐ Drivers License	☐ Known Personally		
☐ Jurat	☐ Passport		Issued Date:	Expiration Date:
☐ Other:	☐ Other:			
Document Type:	Date/Time Notarized: AM PM		Document Date:	Fee Charged:

Printed Name and Address of Witness:	Witness' Signature:
1.	1.
2.	2.

Comments :	Record Number:

NOTARY RECORD

Printed Name and Address of Signer:	Phone Number:	Thumb Print:
	Email:	
	Signer's Signature:	

Service Performed:	Identification:		I.D. Number:	
☐ Oath	☐ I.D Card	☐ Credible Witness	Issued By:	
☐ Acknowledgment	☐ Drivers License	☐ Known Personally		
☐ Jurat	☐ Passport		Issued Date:	Expiration Date:
☐ Other:	☐ Other:			
Document Type:	Date/Time Notarized: AM PM		Document Date:	Fee Charged:

Printed Name and Address of Witness:	Witness' Signature:
1.	1.
2.	2

Comments :	Record Number:

NOTARY RECORD

Printed Name and Address of Signer:

Phone Number:

Email:

Signer's Signature:

Thumb Print:

Service Performed:

- ☐ Oath
- ☐ Acknowledgment
- ☐ Jurat
- ☐ Other:

Identification:

- ☐ I.D Card
- ☐ Credible Witness
- ☐ Drivers License
- ☐ Known Personally
- ☐ Passport
- ☐ Other:

I.D. Number:

Issued By:

Issued Date:

Expiration Date:

Document Type:

Date/Time Notarized: **AM** **PM**

Document Date:

Fee Charged:

Printed Name and Address of Witness:

1.

2.

Witness' Signature:

1.

2.

Comments :

Record Number:

NOTARY RECORD

Printed Name and Address of Signer:

Phone Number:

Email:

Signer's Signature:

Thumb Print:

Service Performed:

- ☐ Oath
- ☐ Acknowledgment
- ☐ Jurat
- ☐ Other:

Identification:

- ☐ I.D Card
- ☐ Credible Witness
- ☐ Drivers License
- ☐ Known Personally
- ☐ Passport
- ☐ Other:

I.D. Number:

Issued By:

Issued Date:

Expiration Date:

Document Type:

Date/Time Notarized: **AM** **PM**

Document Date:

Fee Charged:

Printed Name and Address of Witness:

1.

2.

Witness' Signature:

1.

2

Comments :

Record Number:

NOTARY RECORD

Printed Name and Address of Signer:	Phone Number:	Thumb Print:
	Email:	
	Signer's Signature:	

Service Performed:	Identification:		I.D. Number:	
☐ Oath	☐ I.D Card	☐ Credible Witness	Issued By:	
☐ Acknowledgment	☐ Drivers License	☐ Known Personally	Issued Date:	Expiration Date:
☐ Jurat	☐ Passport			
☐ Other:	☐ Other:			
Document Type:	Date/Time Notarized: AM PM		Document Date:	Fee Charged:

Printed Name and Address of Witness:	Witness' Signature:
1.	1.
2.	2.

Comments :	Record Number:

NOTARY RECORD

Printed Name and Address of Signer:	Phone Number:	Thumb Print:
	Email:	
	Signer's Signature:	

Service Performed:	Identification:		I.D. Number:	
☐ Oath	☐ I.D Card	☐ Credible Witness	Issued By:	
☐ Acknowledgment	☐ Drivers License	☐ Known Personally	Issued Date:	Expiration Date:
☐ Jurat	☐ Passport			
☐ Other:	☐ Other:			
Document Type:	Date/Time Notarized: AM PM		Document Date:	Fee Charged:

Printed Name and Address of Witness:	Witness' Signature:
1.	1.
2.	2

Comments :	Record Number:

NOTARY RECORD

Printed Name and Address of Signer:	**Phone Number:**	**Thumb Print:**
	Email:	
	Signer's Signature:	

Service Performed: ☐ Oath ☐ Acknowledgment ☐ Jurat ☐ Other:	**Identification:** ☐ I.D Card ☐ Credible Witness ☐ Drivers License ☐ Known Personally ☐ Passport ☐ Other:	**I.D. Number:**	
		Issued By:	
		Issued Date:	**Expiration Date:**
Document Type:	**Date/Time Notarized:** AM PM	**Document Date:**	**Fee Charged:**

Printed Name and Address of Witness: **1.** **2.**	**Witness' Signature:** **1.** **2.**
Comments :	**Record Number:**

NOTARY RECORD

Printed Name and Address of Signer:	**Phone Number:**	**Thumb Print:**
	Email:	
	Signer's Signature:	

Service Performed: ☐ Oath ☐ Acknowledgment ☐ Jurat ☐ Other:	**Identification:** ☐ I.D Card ☐ Credible Witness ☐ Drivers License ☐ Known Personally ☐ Passport ☐ Other:	**I.D. Number:**	
		Issued By:	
		Issued Date:	**Expiration Date:**
Document Type:	**Date/Time Notarized:** AM PM	**Document Date:**	**Fee Charged:**

Printed Name and Address of Witness: **1.** **2.**	**Witness' Signature:** **1.** **2**
Comments :	**Record Number:**

NOTARY RECORD

Printed Name and Address of Signer:	Phone Number:	Thumb Print:
	Email:	
	Signer's Signature:	

Service Performed:	Identification:		I.D. Number:	
☐ Oath	☐ I.D Card	☐ Credible Witness		
☐ Acknowlecgment	☐ Drivers License	☐ Known Personally	Issued By:	
☐ Jurat	☐ Passport			
☐ Other:	☐ Other:		Issued Date:	Expiration Date:
Document Type:	Date/Time Notarized: AM PM		Document Date:	Fee Charged:

Printed Name and Address of Witness:	Witness' Signature:
1.	1.
2.	2.

Comments :	Record Number:

NOTARY RECORD

Printed Name and Address of Signer:	Phone Number:	Thumb Print:
	Email:	
	Signer's Signature:	

Service Performed:	Identification:		I.D. Number:	
☐ Oath	☐ I.D Card	☐ Credible Witness		
☐ Acknowledgment	☐ Drivers License	☐ Known Personally	Issued By:	
☐ Jurat	☐ Passport			
☐ Other:	☐ Other:		Issued Date:	Expiration Date:
Document Type:	Date/Time Notarized: AM PM		Document Date:	Fee Charged:

Printed Name and Address of Witness:	Witness' Signature:
1.	1.
2.	2

Comments :	Record Number:

NOTARY RECORD

Printed Name and Address of Signer:	**Phone Number:**	**Thumb Print:**
	Email:	
	Signer's Signature:	

Service Performed: ☐ Oath ☐ Acknowledgment ☐ Jurat ☐ Other:	**Identification:** ☐ I.D Card ☐ Credible Witness ☐ Drivers License ☐ Known Personally ☐ Passport ☐ Other:	**I.D. Number:**	
		Issued By:	
		Issued Date:	**Expiration Date:**
Document Type:	**Date/Time Notarized:** AM PM	**Document Date:**	**Fee Charged:**

Printed Name and Address of Witness: **1.** **2.**	**Witness' Signature:** **1.** **2.**
Comments :	**Record Number:**

NOTARY RECORD

Printed Name and Address of Signer:	**Phone Number:**	**Thumb Print:**
	Email:	
	Signer's Signature:	

Service Performed: ☐ Oath ☐ Acknowledgment ☐ Jurat ☐ Other:	**Identification:** ☐ I.D Card ☐ Credible Witness ☐ Drivers License ☐ Known Personally ☐ Passport ☐ Other:	**I.D. Number:**	
		Issued By:	
		Issued Date:	**Expiration Date:**
Document Type:	**Date/Time Notarized:** AM PM	**Document Date:**	**Fee Charged:**

Printed Name and Address of Witness: **1.** **2.**	**Witness' Signature:** **1.** **2**
Comments :	**Record Number:**

NOTARY RECORD

Printed Name and Address of Signer:	**Phone Number:**	**Thumb Print:**
	Email:	
	Signer's Signature:	

Service Performed: ☐ Oath ☐ Acknowledgment ☐ Jurat ☐ Other:	**Identification:** ☐ I.D Card ☐ Credible Witness ☐ Drivers License ☐ Known Personally ☐ Passport ☐ Other:	**I.D. Number:**	
		Issued By:	
		Issued Date:	**Expiration Date:**
Document Type:	**Date/Time Notarized:** AM PM	**Document Date:**	**Fee Charged:**

Printed Name and Address of Witness: **1.** **2.**	**Witness' Signature:** **1.** **2.**
Comments :	**Record Number:**

NOTARY RECORD

Printed Name and Address of Signer:	**Phone Number:**	**Thumb Print:**
	Email:	
	Signer's Signature:	

Service Performed: ☐ Oath ☐ Acknowledgment ☐ Jurat ☐ Other:	**Identification:** ☐ I.D Card ☐ Credible Witness ☐ Drivers License ☐ Known Personally ☐ Passport ☐ Other:	**I.D. Number:**	
		Issued By:	
		Issued Date:	**Expiration Date:**
Document Type:	**Date/Time Notarized:** AM PM	**Document Date:**	**Fee Charged:**

Printed Name and Address of Witness: **1.** **2.**	**Witness' Signature:** **1.** **2**
Comments :	**Record Number:**

NOTARY RECORD

Printed Name and Address of Signer:	Phone Number:	Thumb Print:
	Email:	
	Signer's Signature:	

Service Performed:	Identification:		I.D. Number:	
☐ Oath	☐ I.D Card	☐ Credible Witness	Issued By:	
☐ Acknowledgment	☐ Drivers License	☐ Known Personally	Issued Date:	Expiration Date:
☐ Jurat	☐ Passport			
☐ Other:	☐ Other:			
Document Type:	Date/Time Notarized: AM PM		Document Date:	Fee Charged:

Printed Name and Address of Witness:	Witness' Signature:
1.	1.
2.	2.

Comments :	Record Number:

NOTARY RECORD

Printed Name and Address of Signer:	Phone Number:	Thumb Print:
	Email:	
	Signer's Signature:	

Service Performed:	Identification:		I.D. Number:	
☐ Oath	☐ I.D Card	☐ Credible Witness	Issued By:	
☐ Acknowledgment	☐ Drivers License	☐ Known Personally	Issued Date:	Expiration Date:
☐ Jurat	☐ Passport			
☐ Other:	☐ Other:			
Document Type:	Date/Time Notarized: AM PM		Document Date:	Fee Charged:

Printed Name and Address of Witness:	Witness' Signature:
1.	1.
2.	2

Comments :	Record Number:

NOTARY RECORD

Printed Name and Address of Signer:	**Phone Number:**	**Thumb Print:**
	Email:	
	Signer's Signature:	

Service Performed: ☐ Oath ☐ Acknowledgment ☐ Jurat ☐ Other:	**Identification:** ☐ I.D Card ☐ Credible Witness ☐ Drivers License ☐ Known Personally ☐ Passport ☐ Other:	**I.D. Number:**	
		Issued By:	
		Issued Date:	**Expiration Date:**
Document Type:	**Date/Time Notarized:** AM PM	**Document Date:**	**Fee Charged:**

Printed Name and Address of Witness: **1.** **2.**	**Witness' Signature:** **1.** **2.**
Comments :	**Record Number:**

NOTARY RECORD

Printed Name and Address of Signer:	**Phone Number:**	**Thumb Print:**
	Email:	
	Signer's Signature:	

Service Performed: ☐ Oath ☐ Acknowledgment ☐ Jurat ☐ Other:	**Identification:** ☐ I.D Card ☐ Credible Witness ☐ Drivers License ☐ Known Personally ☐ Passport ☐ Other:	**I.D. Number:**	
		Issued By:	
		Issued Date:	**Expiration Date:**
Document Type:	**Date/Time Notarized:** AM PM	**Document Date:**	**Fee Charged:**

Printed Name and Address of Witness: **1.** **2.**	**Witness' Signature:** **1.** **2**
Comments :	**Record Number:**

NOTARY RECORD

Printed Name and Address of Signer:	Phone Number:	Thumb Print:
	Email:	
	Signer's Signature:	

Service Performed:	Identification:		I.D. Number:	
☐ Oath	☐ I.D Card	☐ Credible Witness	Issued By:	
☐ Acknowledgment	☐ Drivers License	☐ Known Personally		
☐ Jurat	☐ Passport		Issued Date:	Expiration Date:
☐ Other:	☐ Other:			
Document Type:	Date/Time Notarized:	AM PM	Document Date:	Fee Charged:

Printed Name and Address of Witness:	Witness' Signature:
1.	1.
2.	2.

Comments :	Record Number:

NOTARY RECORD

Printed Name and Address of Signer:	Phone Number:	Thumb Print:
	Email:	
	Signer's Signature:	

Service Performed:	Identification:		I.D. Number:	
☐ Oath	☐ I.D Card	☐ Credible Witness	Issued By:	
☐ Acknowledgment	☐ Drivers License	☐ Known Personally		
☐ Jurat	☐ Passport		Issued Date:	Expiration Date:
☐ Other:	☐ Other:			
Document Type:	Date/Time Notarized:	AM PM	Document Date:	Fee Charged:

Printed Name and Address of Witness:	Witness' Signature:
1.	1.
2.	2

Comments :	Record Number:

NOTARY RECORD

Printed Name and Address of Signer:	Phone Number:	Thumb Print:
	Email:	
	Signer's Signature:	

Service Performed:	Identification:		I.D. Number:	
☐ Oath	☐ I.D Card	☐ Credible Witness	Issued By:	
☐ Acknowledgment	☐ Drivers License	☐ Known Personally	Issued Date:	Expiration Date:
☐ Jurat	☐ Passport			
☐ Other:	☐ Other:			
Document Type:	Date/Time Notarized: AM PM		Document Date:	Fee Charged:

Printed Name and Address of Witness:	Witness' Signature:
1.	1.
2.	2.

Comments :	Record Number:

NOTARY RECORD

Printed Name and Address of Signer:	Phone Number:	Thumb Print:
	Email:	
	Signer's Signature:	

Service Performed:	Identification:		I.D. Number:	
☐ Oath	☐ I.D Card	☐ Credible Witness	Issued By:	
☐ Acknowledgment	☐ Drivers License	☐ Known Personally	Issued Date:	Expiration Date:
☐ Jurat	☐ Passport			
☐ Other:	☐ Other:			
Document Type:	Date/Time Notarized: AM PM		Document Date:	Fee Charged:

Printed Name and Address of Witness:	Witness' Signature:
1.	1.
2.	2

Comments :	Record Number:

NOTARY RECORD

Printed Name and Address of Signer:

Phone Number:

Email:

Signer's Signature:

Thumb Print:

Service Performed:

- ☐ Oath
- ☐ Acknowledgment
- ☐ Jurat
- ☐ Other:

Identification:

- ☐ I.D Card
- ☐ Credible Witness
- ☐ Drivers License
- ☐ Known Personally
- ☐ Passport
- ☐ Other:

I.D. Number:

Issued By:

Issued Date:

Expiration Date:

Document Type:

Date/Time Notarized: AM PM

Document Date:

Fee Charged:

Printed Name and Address of Witness:

1.

2.

Witness' Signature:

1.

2.

Comments :

Record Number:

NOTARY RECORD

Printed Name and Address of Signer:

Phone Number:

Email:

Signer's Signature:

Thumb Print:

Service Performed:

- ☐ Oath
- ☐ Acknowledgment
- ☐ Jurat
- ☐ Other:

Identification:

- ☐ I.D Card
- ☐ Credible Witness
- ☐ Drivers License
- ☐ Known Personally
- ☐ Passport
- ☐ Other:

I.D. Number:

Issued By:

Issued Date:

Expiration Date:

Document Type:

Date/Time Notarized: AM PM

Document Date:

Fee Charged:

Printed Name and Address of Witness:

1.

2.

Witness' Signature:

1.

2

Comments :

Record Number:

NOTARY RECORD

Printed Name and Address of Signer:

Phone Number:

Email:

Signer's Signature:

Thumb Print:

Service Performed:

- ☐ Oath
- ☐ Acknowledgment
- ☐ Jurat
- ☐ Other:

Identification:

- ☐ I.D Card
- ☐ Credible Witness
- ☐ Drivers License
- ☐ Known Personally
- ☐ Passport
- ☐ Other:

I.D. Number:

Issued By:

Issued Date:

Expiration Date:

Document Type:

Date/Time Notarized: **AM** **PM**

Document Date:

Fee Charged:

Printed Name and Address of Witness:

1.

2.

Witness' Signature:

1.

2.

Comments :

Record Number:

NOTARY RECORD

Printed Name and Address of Signer:

Phone Number:

Email:

Signer's Signature:

Thumb Print:

Service Performed:

- ☐ Oath
- ☐ Acknowledgment
- ☐ Jurat
- ☐ Other:

Identification:

- ☐ I.D Card
- ☐ Credible Witness
- ☐ Drivers License
- ☐ Known Personally
- ☐ Passport
- ☐ Other:

I.D. Number:

Issued By:

Issued Date:

Expiration Date:

Document Type:

Date/Time Notarized: **AM** **PM**

Document Date:

Fee Charged:

Printed Name and Address of Witness:

1.

2.

Witness' Signature:

1.

2

Comments :

Record Number:

NOTARY RECORD

Printed Name and Address of Signer:	Phone Number:	Thumb Print:
	Email:	
	Signer's Signature:	

Service Performed:	Identification:		I.D. Number:	
☐ Oath	☐ I.D Card	☐ Credible Witness	Issued By:	
☐ Acknowledgment	☐ Drivers License	☐ Known Personally		
☐ Jurat	☐ Passport		Issued Date:	Expiration Date:
☐ Other:	☐ Other:			
Document Type:	Date/Time Notarized:	AM PM	Document Date:	Fee Charged:

Printed Name and Address of Witness:	Witness' Signature:
1.	1.
2.	2.

Comments :	Record Number:

NOTARY RECORD

Printed Name and Address of Signer:	Phone Number:	Thumb Print:
	Email:	
	Signer's Signature:	

Service Performed:	Identification:		I.D. Number:	
☐ Oath	☐ I.D Card	☐ Credible Witness	Issued By:	
☐ Acknowledgment	☐ Drivers License	☐ Known Personally		
☐ Jurat	☐ Passport		Issued Date:	Expiration Date:
☐ Other:	☐ Other:			
Document Type:	Date/Time Notarized:	AM PM	Document Date:	Fee Charged:

Printed Name and Address of Witness:	Witness' Signature:
1.	1.
2.	2

Comments :	Record Number:

NOTARY RECORD

Printed Name and Address of Signer:	Phone Number:	Thumb Print:
	Email:	
	Signer's Signature:	

Service Performed:	Identification:		I.D. Number:	
☐ Oath	☐ I.D Card	☐ Credible Witness	Issued By:	
☐ Acknowledgment	☐ Drivers License	☐ Known Personally	Issued Date:	Expiration Date:
☐ Jurat	☐ Passport			
☐ Other:	☐ Other:			
Document Type:	Date/Time Notarized:	AM PM	Document Date:	Fee Charged:

Printed Name and Address of Witness:	Witness' Signature:
1.	1.
2.	2.

Comments :	Record Number:

NOTARY RECORD

Printed Name and Address of Signer:	Phone Number:	Thumb Print:
	Email:	
	Signer's Signature:	

Service Performed:	Identification:		I.D. Number:	
☐ Oath	☐ I.D Card	☐ Credible Witness	Issued By:	
☐ Acknowledgment	☐ Drivers License	☐ Known Personally	Issued Date:	Expiration Date:
☐ Jurat	☐ Passport			
☐ Other:	☐ Other:			
Document Type:	Date/Time Notarized:	AM PM	Document Date:	Fee Charged:

Printed Name and Address of Witness:	Witness' Signature:
1.	1.
2.	2

Comments :	Record Number:

NOTARY RECORD

Printed Name and Address of Signer:

Phone Number:

Email:

Signer's Signature:

Thumb Print:

Service Performed:

- ☐ Oath
- ☐ Acknowledgment
- ☐ Jurat
- ☐ Other:

Identification:

- ☐ I.D Card
- ☐ Credible Witness
- ☐ Drivers License
- ☐ Known Personally
- ☐ Passport
- ☐ Other:

I.D. Number:

Issued By:

Issued Date:

Expiration Date:

Document Type:

Date/Time Notarized: **AM** **PM**

Document Date:

Fee Charged:

Printed Name and Address of Witness:

1.

2.

Witness' Signature:

1.

2.

Comments :

Record Number:

NOTARY RECORD

Printed Name and Address of Signer:

Phone Number:

Email:

Signer's Signature:

Thumb Print:

Service Performed:

- ☐ Oath
- ☐ Acknowledgment
- ☐ Jurat
- ☐ Other:

Identification:

- ☐ I.D Card
- ☐ Credible Witness
- ☐ Drivers License
- ☐ Known Personally
- ☐ Passport
- ☐ Other:

I.D. Number:

Issued By:

Issued Date:

Expiration Date:

Document Type:

Date/Time Notarized: **AM** **PM**

Document Date:

Fee Charged:

Printed Name and Address of Witness:

1.

2.

Witness' Signature:

1.

2

Comments :

Record Number:

NOTARY RECORD

Printed Name and Address of Signer:	Phone Number:	Thumb Print:
	Email:	
	Signer's Signature:	

Service Performed:	Identification:		I.D. Number:	
☐ Oath	☐ I.D Card	☐ Credible Witness		
☐ Acknowledgment	☐ Drivers License	☐ Known Personally	Issued By:	
☐ Jurat	☐ Passport			
☐ Other:	☐ Other:		Issued Date:	Expiration Date:

Document Type:	Date/Time Notarized: AM PM	Document Date:	Fee Charged:

Printed Name and Address of Witness:	Witness' Signature:
1.	1.
2.	2.

Comments :	Record Number:

NOTARY RECORD

Printed Name and Address of Signer:	Phone Number:	Thumb Print:
	Email:	
	Signer's Signature:	

Service Performed:	Identification:		I.D. Number:	
☐ Oath	☐ I.D Card	☐ Credible Witness		
☐ Acknowledgment	☐ Drivers License	☐ Known Personally	Issued By:	
☐ Jurat	☐ Passport			
☐ Other:	☐ Other:		Issued Date:	Expiration Date:

Document Type:	Date/Time Notarized: AM PM	Document Date:	Fee Charged:

Printed Name and Address of Witness:	Witness' Signature:
1.	1.
2.	2

Comments :	Record Number:

NOTARY RECORD

Printed Name and Address of Signer:	Phone Number:	Thumb Print:
	Email:	
	Signer's Signature:	

Service Performed:	Identification:		I.D. Number:	
☐ Oath	☐ I.D Card	☐ Credible Witness	Issued By:	
☐ Acknowledgment	☐ Drivers License	☐ Known Personally	Issued Date:	Expiration Date:
☐ Jurat	☐ Passport			
☐ Other:	☐ Other:			
Document Type:	Date/Time Notarized:	AM PM	Document Date:	Fee Charged:

Printed Name and Address of Witness:	Witness' Signature:
1.	1.
2.	2.

Comments :	Record Number:

NOTARY RECORD

Printed Name and Address of Signer:	Phone Number:	Thumb Print:
	Email:	
	Signer's Signature:	

Service Performed:	Identification:		I.D. Number:	
☐ Oath	☐ I.D Card	☐ Credible Witness	Issued By:	
☐ Acknowledgment	☐ Drivers License	☐ Known Personally	Issued Date:	Expiration Date:
☐ Jurat	☐ Passport			
☐ Other:	☐ Other:			
Document Type:	Date/Time Notarized:	AM PM	Document Date:	Fee Charged:

Printed Name and Address of Witness:	Witness' Signature:
1.	1.
2.	2

Comments :	Record Number:

NOTARY RECORD

Printed Name and Address of Signer:	**Phone Number:**	**Thumb Print:**
	Email:	
	Signer's Signature:	

Service Performed: ☐ Oath ☐ Acknowledgment ☐ Jurat ☐ Other:	**Identification:** ☐ I.D Card ☐ Credible Witness ☐ Drivers License ☐ Known Personally ☐ Passport ☐ Other:	**I.D. Number:**	
		Issued By:	
		Issued Date:	**Expiration Date:**
Document Type:	**Date/Time Notarized:** **AM** **PM**	**Document Date:**	**Fee Charged:**

Printed Name and Address of Witness: **1.** **2.**	**Witness' Signature:** **1.** **2.**

Comments :	**Record Number:**

NOTARY RECORD

Printed Name and Address of Signer:	**Phone Number:**	**Thumb Print:**
	Email:	
	Signer's Signature:	

Service Performed: ☐ Oath ☐ Acknowledgment ☐ Jurat ☐ Other:	**Identification:** ☐ I.D Card ☐ Credible Witness ☐ Drivers License ☐ Known Personally ☐ Passport ☐ Other:	**I.D. Number:**	
		Issued By:	
		Issued Date:	**Expiration Date:**
Document Type:	**Date/Time Notarized:** **AM** **PM**	**Document Date:**	**Fee Charged:**

Printed Name and Address of Witness: **1.** **2.**	**Witness' Signature:** **1.** **2**

Comments :	**Record Number:**

NOTARY RECORD

Printed Name and Address of Signer:	Phone Number:	Thumb Print:
	Email:	
	Signer's Signature:	

Service Performed:	Identification:		I.D. Number:	
☐ Oath	☐ I.D Card	☐ Credible Witness	Issued By:	
☐ Acknowledgment	☐ Drivers License	☐ Known Personally	Issued Date:	Expiration Date:
☐ Jurat	☐ Passport			
☐ Other:	☐ Other:			
Document Type:	Date/Time Notarized:	AM PM	Document Date:	Fee Charged:

Printed Name and Address of Witness:	Witness' Signature:
1.	1.
2.	2.

Comments :	Record Number:

NOTARY RECORD

Printed Name and Address of Signer:	Phone Number:	Thumb Print:
	Email:	
	Signer's Signature:	

Service Performed:	Identification:		I.D. Number:	
☐ Oath	☐ I.D Card	☐ Credible Witness	Issued By:	
☐ Acknowledgment	☐ Drivers License	☐ Known Personally	Issued Date:	Expiration Date:
☐ Jurat	☐ Passport			
☐ Other:	☐ Other:			
Document Type:	Date/Time Notarized:	AM PM	Document Date:	Fee Charged:

Printed Name and Address of Witness:	Witness' Signature:
1.	1.
2.	2

Comments :	Record Number:

NOTARY RECORD

Printed Name and Address of Signer:	Phone Number:	Thumb Print:
	Email:	
	Signer's Signature:	

Service Performed:	Identification:		I.D. Number:	
☐ Oath	☐ I.D Card	☐ Credible Witness		
☐ Acknowledgment	☐ Drivers License	☐ Known Personally	Issued By:	
☐ Jurat	☐ Passport			
☐ Other:	☐ Other:		Issued Date:	Expiration Date:
Document Type:	Date/Time Notarized:	AM PM	Document Date:	Fee Charged:

Printed Name and Address of Witness:	Witness' Signature:
1.	1.
2.	2.

Comments :	Record Number:

NOTARY RECORD

Printed Name and Address of Signer:	Phone Number:	Thumb Print:
	Email:	
	Signer's Signature:	

Service Performed:	Identification:		I.D. Number:	
☐ Oath	☐ I.D Card	☐ Credible Witness		
☐ Acknowledgment	☐ Drivers License	☐ Known Personally	Issued By:	
☐ Jurat	☐ Passport			
☐ Other:	☐ Other:		Issued Date:	Expiration Date:
Document Type:	Date/Time Notarized:	AM PM	Document Date:	Fee Charged:

Printed Name and Address of Witness:	Witness' Signature:
1.	1.
2.	2

Comments :	Record Number:

NOTARY RECORD

Printed Name and Address of Signer:	**Phone Number:**	**Thumb Print:**
	Email:	
	Signer's Signature:	

Service Performed: ☐ Oath ☐ Acknowledgment ☐ Jurat ☐ Other:	**Identification:** ☐ I.D Card ☐ Credible Witness ☐ Drivers License ☐ Known Personally ☐ Passport ☐ Other:	**I.D. Number:**	
		Issued By:	
		Issued Date:	**Expiration Date:**
Document Type:	**Date/Time Notarized:** AM PM	**Document Date:**	**Fee Charged:**

Printed Name and Address of Witness: **1.** **2.**	**Witness' Signature:** **1.** **2.**
Comments :	**Record Number:**

NOTARY RECORD

Printed Name and Address of Signer:	**Phone Number:**	**Thumb Print:**
	Email:	
	Signer's Signature:	

Service Performed: ☐ Oath ☐ Acknowledgment ☐ Jurat ☐ Other:	**Identification:** ☐ I.D Card ☐ Credible Witness ☐ Drivers License ☐ Known Personally ☐ Passport ☐ Other:	**I.D. Number:**	
		Issued By:	
		Issued Date:	**Expiration Date:**
Document Type:	**Date/Time Notarized:** AM PM	**Document Date:**	**Fee Charged:**

Printed Name and Address of Witness: **1.** **2.**	**Witness' Signature:** **1.** **2**

Comments :	**Record Number:**

NOTARY RECORD

Printed Name and Address of Signer:	Phone Number:	Thumb Print:
	Email:	
	Signer's Signature:	

Service Performed:	Identification:		I.D. Number:	
☐ Oath	☐ I.D Card	☐ Credible Witness	Issued By:	
☐ Acknowledgment	☐ Drivers License	☐ Known Personally	Issued Date:	Expiration Date:
☐ Jurat	☐ Passport			
☐ Other:	☐ Other:			
Document Type:	Date/Time Notarized: AM PM		Document Date:	Fee Charged:

Printed Name and Address of Witness:	Witness' Signature:
1.	1.
2.	2.

Comments :	Record Number:

NOTARY RECORD

Printed Name and Address of Signer:	Phone Number:	Thumb Print:
	Email:	
	Signer's Signature:	

Service Performed:	Identification:		I.D. Number:	
☐ Oath	☐ I.D Card	☐ Credible Witness	Issued By:	
☐ Acknowledgment	☐ Drivers License	☐ Known Personally	Issued Date:	Expiration Date:
☐ Jurat	☐ Passport			
☐ Other:	☐ Other:			
Document Type:	Date/Time Notarized: AM PM		Document Date:	Fee Charged:

Printed Name and Address of Witness:	Witness' Signature:
1.	1.
2.	2

Comments :	Record Number:

NOTARY RECORD

Printed Name and Address of Signer:	Phone Number:	Thumb Print:
	Email:	
	Signer's Signature:	

Service Performed:	Identification:		I.D. Number:	
☐ Oath	☐ I.D Card	☐ Credible Witness		
☐ Acknowledgment	☐ Drivers License	☐ Known Personally	Issued By:	
☐ Jurat	☐ Passport			
☐ Other:	☐ Other:		Issued Date:	Expiration Date:
Document Type:	Date/Time Notarized: AM PM		Document Date:	Fee Charged:

Printed Name and Address of Witness:	Witness' Signature:
1.	1.
2.	2.

Comments :	Record Number:

NOTARY RECORD

Printed Name and Address of Signer:	Phone Number:	Thumb Print:
	Email:	
	Signer's Signature:	

Service Performed:	Identification:		I.D. Number:	
☐ Oath	☐ I.D Card	☐ Credible Witness		
☐ Acknowledgment	☐ Drivers License	☐ Known Personally	Issued By:	
☐ Jurat	☐ Passport			
☐ Other:	☐ Other:		Issued Date:	Expiration Date:
Document Type:	Date/Time Notarized: AM PM		Document Date:	Fee Charged:

Printed Name and Address of Witness:	Witness' Signature:
1.	1.
2.	2

Comments :	Record Number:

NOTARY RECORD

Printed Name and Address of Signer:	**Phone Number:**	**Thumb Print:**
	Email:	
	Signer's Signature:	

Service Performed: ☐ Oath ☐ Acknowledgment ☐ Jurat ☐ Other:	**Identification:** ☐ I.D Card ☐ Credible Witness ☐ Drivers License ☐ Known Personally ☐ Passport ☐ Other:	**I.D. Number:**	
		Issued By:	
		Issued Date:	**Expiration Date:**
Document Type:	**Date/Time Notarized:** **AM** **PM**	**Document Date:**	**Fee Charged:**

Printed Name and Address of Witness: **1.** **2.**	**Witness' Signature:** **1.** **2.**

Comments :	**Record Number:**

NOTARY RECORD

Printed Name and Address of Signer:	**Phone Number:**	**Thumb Print:**
	Email:	
	Signer's Signature:	

Service Performed: ☐ Oath ☐ Acknowledgment ☐ Jurat ☐ Other:	**Identification:** ☐ I.D Card ☐ Credible Witness ☐ Drivers License ☐ Known Personally ☐ Passport ☐ Other:	**I.D. Number:**	
		Issued By:	
		Issued Date:	**Expiration Date:**
Document Type:	**Date/Time Notarized:** **AM** **PM**	**Document Date:**	**Fee Charged:**

Printed Name and Address of Witness: **1.** **2.**	**Witness' Signature:** **1.** **2**

Comments :	**Record Number:**

NOTARY RECORD

Printed Name and Address of Signer:	Phone Number:	Thumb Print:
	Email:	
	Signer's Signature:	

Service Performed:	Identification:		I.D. Number:	
☐ Oath	☐ I.D Card	☐ Credible Witness		
☐ Acknowledgment	☐ Drivers License	☐ Known Personally	Issued By:	
☐ Jurat	☐ Passport			
☐ Other:	☐ Other:		Issued Date:	Expiration Date:
Document Type:	Date/Time Notarized: AM PM		Document Date:	Fee Charged:

Printed Name and Address of Witness:	Witness' Signature:
1.	1.
2.	2.

Comments :	Record Number:

NOTARY RECORD

Printed Name and Address of Signer:	Phone Number:	Thumb Print:
	Email:	
	Signer's Signature:	

Service Performed:	Identification:		I.D. Number:	
☐ Oath	☐ I.D Card	☐ Credible Witness		
☐ Acknowledgment	☐ Drivers License	☐ Known Personally	Issued By:	
☐ Jurat	☐ Passport			
☐ Other:	☐ Other:		Issued Date:	Expiration Date:
Document Type:	Date/Time Notarized: AM PM		Document Date:	Fee Charged:

Printed Name and Address of Witness:	Witness' Signature:
1.	1.
2.	2

Comments :	Record Number:

NOTARY RECORD

Printed Name and Address of Signer:	Phone Number:	Thumb Print:
	Email:	
	Signer's Signature:	

Service Performed:	Identification:		I.D. Number:	
☐ Oath	☐ I.D Card	☐ Credible Witness		
☐ Acknowledgment	☐ Drivers License	☐ Known Personally	Issued By:	
☐ Jurat	☐ Passport			
☐ Other:	☐ Other:		Issued Date:	Expiration Date:
Document Type:	Date/Time Notarized:	AM PM	Document Date:	Fee Charged:

Printed Name and Address of Witness:	Witness' Signature:
1.	1.
2.	2.

Comments :	Record Number:

NOTARY RECORD

Printed Name and Address of Signer:	Phone Number:	Thumb Print:
	Email:	
	Signer's Signature:	

Service Performed:	Identification:		I.D. Number:	
☐ Oath	☐ I.D Card	☐ Credible Witness		
☐ Acknowledgment	☐ Drivers License	☐ Known Personally	Issued By:	
☐ Jurat	☐ Passport			
☐ Other:	☐ Other:		Issued Date:	Expiration Date:
Document Type:	Date/Time Notarized:	AM PM	Document Date:	Fee Charged:

Printed Name and Address of Witness:	Witness' Signature:
1.	1.
2.	2

Comments :	Record Number:

NOTARY RECORD

Printed Name and Address of Signer:	**Phone Number:**	**Thumb Print:**
	Email:	
	Signer's Signature:	

Service Performed: ☐ Oath ☐ Acknowledgment ☐ Jurat ☐ Other:	**Identification:** ☐ I.D Card ☐ Credible Witness ☐ Drivers License ☐ Known Personally ☐ Passport ☐ Other:	**I.D. Number:**	
		Issued By:	
		Issued Date:	**Expiration Date:**
Document Type:	**Date/Time Notarized:** AM PM	**Document Date:**	**Fee Charged:**

Printed Name and Address of Witness: **1.** **2.**	**Witness' Signature:** **1.** **2.**
Comments :	**Record Number:**

NOTARY RECORD

Printed Name and Address of Signer:	**Phone Number:**	**Thumb Print:**
	Email:	
	Signer's Signature:	

Service Performed: ☐ Oath ☐ Acknowledgment ☐ Jurat ☐ Other:	**Identification:** ☐ I.D Card ☐ Credible Witness ☐ Drivers License ☐ Known Personally ☐ Passport ☐ Other:	**I.D. Number:**	
		Issued By:	
		Issued Date:	**Expiration Date:**
Document Type:	**Date/Time Notarized:** AM PM	**Document Date:**	**Fee Charged:**

Printed Name and Address of Witness: **1.** **2.**	**Witness' Signature:** **1.** **2**
Comments :	**Record Number:**

NOTARY RECORD

Printed Name and Address of Signer:	Phone Number:	Thumb Print:
	Email:	
	Signer's Signature:	

Service Performed:	Identification:		I.D. Number:	
☐ Oath	☐ I.D Card	☐ Credible Witness	Issued By:	
☐ Acknowledgment	☐ Drivers License	☐ Known Personally		
☐ Jurat	☐ Passport		Issued Date:	Expiration Date:
☐ Other:	☐ Other:			
Document Type:	Date/Time Notarized: AM PM		Document Date:	Fee Charged:

Printed Name and Address of Witness:	Witness' Signature:
1.	1.
2.	2.

Comments :	Record Number:

NOTARY RECORD

Printed Name and Address of Signer:	Phone Number:	Thumb Print:
	Email:	
	Signer's Signature:	

Service Performed:	Identification:		I.D. Number:	
☐ Oath	☐ I.D Card	☐ Credible Witness	Issued By:	
☐ Acknowledgment	☐ Drivers License	☐ Known Personally		
☐ Jurat	☐ Passport		Issued Date:	Expiration Date:
☐ Other:	☐ Other:			
Document Type:	Date/Time Notarized: AM PM		Document Date:	Fee Charged:

Printed Name and Address of Witness:	Witness' Signature:
1.	1.
2.	2

Comments :	Record Number:

NOTARY RECORD

Printed Name and Address of Signer:

Phone Number:

Email:

Signer's Signature:

Thumb Print:

Service Performed:

- ☐ Oath
- ☐ Acknowledgment
- ☐ Jurat
- ☐ Other:

Identification:

- ☐ I.D Card
- ☐ Credible Witness
- ☐ Drivers License
- ☐ Known Personally
- ☐ Passport
- ☐ Other:

I.D. Number:

Issued By:

Issued Date:

Expiration Date:

Document Type:

Date/Time Notarized: **AM** **PM**

Document Date:

Fee Charged:

Printed Name and Address of Witness:

1.

2.

Witness' Signature:

1.

2.

Comments :

Record Number:

NOTARY RECORD

Printed Name and Address of Signer:

Phone Number:

Email:

Signer's Signature:

Thumb Print:

Service Performed:

- ☐ Oath
- ☐ Acknowledgment
- ☐ Jurat
- ☐ Other:

Identification:

- ☐ I.D Card
- ☐ Credible Witness
- ☐ Drivers License
- ☐ Known Personally
- ☐ Passport
- ☐ Other:

I.D. Number:

Issued By:

Issued Date:

Expiration Date:

Document Type:

Date/Time Notarized: **AM** **PM**

Document Date:

Fee Charged:

Printed Name and Address of Witness:

1.

2.

Witness' Signature:

1.

2

Comments :

Record Number:

NOTARY RECORD

Printed Name and Address of Signer:	Phone Number:	Thumb Print:
	Email:	
	Signer's Signature:	

Service Performed:	Identification:		I.D. Number:	
☐ Oath	☐ I.D Card	☐ Credible Witness		
☐ Acknowledgment	☐ Drivers License	☐ Known Personally	Issued By:	
☐ Jurat	☐ Passport			
☐ Other:	☐ Other:		Issued Date:	Expiration Date:
Document Type:	Date/Time Notarized: AM PM		Document Date:	Fee Charged:

Printed Name and Address of Witness:	Witness' Signature:
1.	1.
2.	2.

Comments :	Record Number:

NOTARY RECORD

Printed Name and Address of Signer:	Phone Number:	Thumb Print:
	Email:	
	Signer's Signature:	

Service Performed:	Identification:		I.D. Number:	
☐ Oath	☐ I.D Card	☐ Credible Witness		
☐ Acknowledgment	☐ Drivers License	☐ Known Personally	Issued By:	
☐ Jurat	☐ Passport			
☐ Other:	☐ Other:		Issued Date:	Expiration Date:
Document Type:	Date/Time Notarized: AM PM		Document Date:	Fee Charged:

Printed Name and Address of Witness:	Witness' Signature:
1.	1.
2.	2

Comments :	Record Number:

NOTARY RECORD

Printed Name and Address of Signer:	Phone Number:	Thumb Print:
	Email:	
	Signer's Signature:	

Service Performed:	Identification:		I.D. Number:	
☐ Oath	☐ I.D Card	☐ Credible Witness		
☐ Acknowledgment	☐ Drivers License	☐ Known Personally	Issued By:	
☐ Jurat	☐ Passport			
☐ Other:	☐ Other:		Issued Date:	Expiration Date:
Document Type:	Date/Time Notarized:	AM PM	Document Date:	Fee Charged:

Printed Name and Address of Witness:	Witness' Signature:
1.	1.
2.	2.

Comments :	Record Number:

NOTARY RECORD

Printed Name and Address of Signer:	Phone Number:	Thumb Print:
	Email:	
	Signer's Signature:	

Service Performed:	Identification:		I.D. Number:	
☐ Oath	☐ I.D Card	☐ Credible Witness		
☐ Acknowledgment	☐ Drivers License	☐ Known Personally	Issued By:	
☐ Jurat	☐ Passport			
☐ Other:	☐ Other:		Issued Date:	Expiration Date:
Document Type:	Date/Time Notarized:	AM PM	Document Date:	Fee Charged:

Printed Name and Address of Witness:	Witness' Signature:
1.	1.
2.	2

Comments :	Record Number:

NOTARY RECORD

Printed Name and Address of Signer:	**Phone Number:** **Email:** **Signer's Signature:**	**Thumb Print:**

Service Performed: ☐ Oath ☐ Acknowledgment ☐ Jurat ☐ Other:	**Identification:** ☐ I.D Card ☐ Credible Witness ☐ Drivers License ☐ Known Personally ☐ Passport ☐ Other:	**I.D. Number:** **Issued By:** **Issued Date:**	**Expiration Date:**
Document Type:	**Date/Time Notarized:** **AM** **PM**	**Document Date:**	**Fee Charged:**

Printed Name and Address of Witness: **1.** **2.**	**Witness' Signature:** **1.** **2.**
Comments :	**Record Number:**

NOTARY RECORD

Printed Name and Address of Signer:	**Phone Number:** **Email:** **Signer's Signature:**	**Thumb Print:**

Service Performed: ☐ Oath ☐ Acknowledgment ☐ Jurat ☐ Other:	**Identification:** ☐ I.D Card ☐ Credible Witness ☐ Drivers License ☐ Known Personally ☐ Passport ☐ Other:	**I.D. Number:** **Issued By:** **Issued Date:**	**Expiration Date:**
Document Type:	**Date/Time Notarized:** **AM** **PM**	**Document Date:**	**Fee Charged:**

Printed Name and Address of Witness: **1.** **2.**	**Witness' Signature:** **1.** **2**
Comments :	**Record Number:**

NOTARY RECORD

Printed Name and Address of Signer:	Phone Number:	Thumb Print:
	Email:	
	Signer's Signature:	

Service Performed:	Identification:		I.D. Number:	
☐ Oath	☐ I.D Card	☐ Credible Witness		
☐ Acknowledgment	☐ Drivers License	☐ Known Personally	Issued By:	
☐ Jurat	☐ Passport			
☐ Other:	☐ Other:		Issued Date:	Expiration Date:
Document Type:	Date/Time Notarized: AM PM		Document Date:	Fee Charged:

Printed Name and Address of Witness:	Witness' Signature:
1.	1.
2.	2.

Comments :	Record Number:

NOTARY RECORD

Printed Name and Address of Signer:	Phone Number:	Thumb Print:
	Email:	
	Signer's Signature:	

Service Performed:	Identification:		I.D. Number:	
☐ Oath	☐ I.D Card	☐ Credible Witness		
☐ Acknowledgment	☐ Drivers License	☐ Known Personally	Issued By:	
☐ Jurat	☐ Passport			
☐ Other:	☐ Other:		Issued Date:	Expiration Date:
Document Type:	Date/Time Notarized: AM PM		Document Date:	Fee Charged:

Printed Name and Address of Witness:	Witness' Signature:
1.	1.
2.	2

Comments :	Record Number:

NOTARY RECORD

Printed Name and Address of Signer:

Phone Number:

Email:

Signer's Signature:

Thumb Print:

Service Performed:

- ☐ Oath
- ☐ Acknowledgment
- ☐ Jurat
- ☐ Other:

Identification:

- ☐ I.D Card
- ☐ Credible Witness
- ☐ Drivers License
- ☐ Known Personally
- ☐ Passport
- ☐ Other:

I.D. Number:

Issued By:

Issued Date:

Expiration Date:

Document Type:

Date/Time Notarized: AM PM

Document Date:

Fee Charged:

Printed Name and Address of Witness:

1.

2.

Witness' Signature:

1.

2.

Comments :

Record Number:

NOTARY RECORD

Printed Name and Address of Signer:

Phone Number:

Email:

Signer's Signature:

Thumb Print:

Service Performed:

- ☐ Oath
- ☐ Acknowledgment
- ☐ Jurat
- ☐ Other:

Identification:

- ☐ I.D Card
- ☐ Credible Witness
- ☐ Drivers License
- ☐ Known Personally
- ☐ Passport
- ☐ Other:

I.D. Number:

Issued By:

Issued Date:

Expiration Date:

Document Type:

Date/Time Notarized: AM PM

Document Date:

Fee Charged:

Printed Name and Address of Witness:

1.

2.

Witness' Signature:

1.

2

Comments :

Record Number:

NOTARY RECORD

Printed Name and Address of Signer:	Phone Number:	Thumb Print:
	Email:	
	Signer's Signature:	

Service Performed:	Identification:		I.D. Number:	
☐ Oath	☐ I.D Card	☐ Credible Witness		
☐ Acknowledgment	☐ Drivers License	☐ Known Personally	Issued By:	
☐ Jurat	☐ Passport			
☐ Other:	☐ Other:		Issued Date:	Expiration Date:
Document Type:	Date/Time Notarized: AM PM		Document Date:	Fee Charged:

Printed Name and Address of Witness:	Witness' Signature:
1.	1.
2.	2.

Comments :	Record Number:

NOTARY RECORD

Printed Name and Address of Signer:	Phone Number:	Thumb Print:
	Email:	
	Signer's Signature:	

Service Performed:	Identification:		I.D. Number:	
☐ Oath	☐ I.D Card	☐ Credible Witness		
☐ Acknowledgment	☐ Drivers License	☐ Known Personally	Issued By:	
☐ Jurat	☐ Passport			
☐ Other:	☐ Other:		Issued Date:	Expiration Date:
Document Type:	Date/Time Notarized: AM PM		Document Date:	Fee Charged:

Printed Name and Address of Witness:	Witness' Signature:
1.	1.
2.	2

Comments :	Record Number:

NOTARY RECORD

Printed Name and Address of Signer:	Phone Number:	Thumb Print:
	Email:	
	Signer's Signature:	

Service Performed:	Identification:		I.D. Number:	
☐ Oath	☐ I.D Card	☐ Credible Witness		
☐ Acknowledgment	☐ Drivers License	☐ Known Personally	Issued By:	
☐ Jurat	☐ Passport			
☐ Other:	☐ Other:		Issued Date:	Expiration Date:
Document Type:	Date/Time Notarized: AM PM		Document Date:	Fee Charged:

Printed Name and Address of Witness:	Witness' Signature:
1.	1.
2.	2.

Comments :	Record Number:

NOTARY RECORD

Printed Name and Address of Signer:	Phone Number:	Thumb Print:
	Email:	
	Signer's Signature:	

Service Performed:	Identification:		I.D. Number:	
☐ Oath	☐ I.D Card	☐ Credible Witness		
☐ Acknowledgment	☐ Drivers License	☐ Known Personally	Issued By:	
☐ Jurat	☐ Passport			
☐ Other:	☐ Other:		Issued Date:	Expiration Date:
Document Type:	Date/Time Notarized: AM PM		Document Date:	Fee Charged:

Printed Name and Address of Witness:	Witness' Signature:
1.	1.
2.	2

Comments :	Record Number:

NOTARY RECORD

Printed Name and Address of Signer:	Phone Number:	Thumb Print:
	Email:	
	Signer's Signature:	

Service Performed:	Identification:		I.D. Number:	
☐ Oath	☐ I.D Card	☐ Credible Witness	Issued By:	
☐ Acknowledgment	☐ Drivers License	☐ Known Personally		
☐ Jurat	☐ Passport		Issued Date:	Expiration Date:
☐ Other:	☐ Other:			
Document Type:	Date/Time Notarized:	AM PM	Document Date:	Fee Charged:

Printed Name and Address of Witness:	Witness' Signature:
1.	1.
2.	2.

Comments :	Record Number:

NOTARY RECORD

Printed Name and Address of Signer:	Phone Number:	Thumb Print:
	Email:	
	Signer's Signature:	

Service Performed:	Identification:		I.D. Number:	
☐ Oath	☐ I.D Card	☐ Credible Witness	Issued By:	
☐ Acknowledgment	☐ Drivers License	☐ Known Personally		
☐ Jurat	☐ Passport		Issued Date:	Expiration Date:
☐ Other:	☐ Other:			
Document Type:	Date/Time Notarized:	AM PM	Document Date:	Fee Charged:

Printed Name and Address of Witness:	Witness' Signature:
1.	1.
2.	2

Comments :	Record Number:

NOTARY RECORD

Printed Name and Address of Signer:	Phone Number:	Thumb Print:
	Email:	
	Signer's Signature:	

Service Performed:	Identification:		I.D. Number:	
☐ Oath	☐ I.D Card	☐ Credible Witness	Issued By:	
☐ Acknowledgment	☐ Drivers License	☐ Known Personally		
☐ Jurat	☐ Passport		Issued Date:	Expiration Date:
☐ Other:	☐ Other:			
Document Type:	Date/Time Notarized: AM PM		Document Date:	Fee Charged:

Printed Name and Address of Witness:	Witness' Signature:
1.	1.
2.	2.

Comments :	Record Number:

NOTARY RECORD

Printed Name and Address of Signer:	Phone Number:	Thumb Print:
	Email:	
	Signer's Signature:	

Service Performed:	Identification:		I.D. Number:	
☐ Oath	☐ I.D Card	☐ Credible Witness	Issued By:	
☐ Acknowledgment	☐ Drivers License	☐ Known Personally		
☐ Jurat	☐ Passport		Issued Date:	Expiration Date:
☐ Other:	☐ Other:			
Document Type:	Date/Time Notarized: AM PM		Document Date:	Fee Charged:

Printed Name and Address of Witness:	Witness' Signature:
1.	1.
2.	2

Comments :	Record Number:

NOTARY RECORD

Printed Name and Address of Signer:	**Phone Number:**	**Thumb Print:**
	Email:	
	Signer's Signature:	

Service Performed: ☐ Oath ☐ Acknowledgment ☐ Jurat ☐ Other:	**Identification:** ☐ I.D Card ☐ Credible Witness ☐ Drivers License ☐ Known Personally ☐ Passport ☐ Other:	**I.D. Number:**	
		Issued By:	
		Issued Date:	**Expiration Date:**
Document Type:	**Date/Time Notarized:** **AM** **PM**	**Document Date:**	**Fee Charged:**

Printed Name and Address of Witness: **1.** **2.**	**Witness' Signature:** **1.** **2.**
Comments :	**Record Number:**

NOTARY RECORD

Printed Name and Address of Signer:	**Phone Number:**	**Thumb Print:**
	Email:	
	Signer's Signature:	

Service Performed: ☐ Oath ☐ Acknowledgment ☐ Jurat ☐ Other:	**Identification:** ☐ I.D Card ☐ Credible Witness ☐ Drivers License ☐ Known Personally ☐ Passport ☐ Other:	**I.D. Number:**	
		Issued By:	
		Issued Date:	**Expiration Date:**
Document Type:	**Date/Time Notarized:** **AM** **PM**	**Document Date:**	**Fee Charged:**

Printed Name and Address of Witness: **1.** **2.**	**Witness' Signature:** **1.** **2**
Comments :	**Record Number:**

NOTARY RECORD

Printed Name and Address of Signer:

Phone Number:

Email:

Signer's Signature:

Thumb Print:

Service Performed:

- ☐ Oath
- ☐ Acknowledgment
- ☐ Jurat
- ☐ Other:

Identification:

- ☐ I.D Card
- ☐ Credible Witness
- ☐ Drivers License
- ☐ Known Personally
- ☐ Passport
- ☐ Other:

I.D. Number:

Issued By:

Issued Date:

Expiration Date:

Document Type:

Date/Time Notarized: **AM** **PM**

Document Date:

Fee Charged:

Printed Name and Address of Witness:

1.

2.

Witness' Signature:

1.

2.

Comments :

Record Number:

NOTARY RECORD

Printed Name and Address of Signer:

Phone Number:

Email:

Signer's Signature:

Thumb Print:

Service Performed:

- ☐ Oath
- ☐ Acknowledgment
- ☐ Jurat
- ☐ Other:

Identification:

- ☐ I.D Card
- ☐ Credible Witness
- ☐ Drivers License
- ☐ Known Personally
- ☐ Passport
- ☐ Other:

I.D. Number:

Issued By:

Issued Date:

Expiration Date:

Document Type:

Date/Time Notarized: **AM** **PM**

Document Date:

Fee Charged:

Printed Name and Address of Witness:

1.

2.

Witness' Signature:

1.

2

Comments :

Record Number:

NOTARY RECORD

Printed Name and Address of Signer:	Phone Number:	Thumb Print:
	Email:	
	Signer's Signature:	

Service Performed:	Identification:		I.D. Number:	
☐ Oath	☐ I.D Card	☐ Credible Witness		
☐ Acknowledgment	☐ Drivers License	☐ Known Personally	Issued By:	
☐ Jurat	☐ Passport			
☐ Other:	☐ Other:		Issued Date:	Expiration Date:
Document Type:	Date/Time Notarized:	AM PM	Document Date:	Fee Charged:

Printed Name and Address of Witness:	Witness' Signature:
1.	1.
2.	2.

Comments :	Record Number:

NOTARY RECORD

Printed Name and Address of Signer:	Phone Number:	Thumb Print:
	Email:	
	Signer's Signature:	

Service Performed:	Identification:		I.D. Number:	
☐ Oath	☐ I.D Card	☐ Credible Witness		
☐ Acknowledgment	☐ Drivers License	☐ Known Personally	Issued By:	
☐ Jurat	☐ Passport			
☐ Other:	☐ Other:		Issued Date:	Expiration Date:
Document Type:	Date/Time Notarized:	AM PM	Document Date:	Fee Charged:

Printed Name and Address of Witness:	Witness' Signature:
1.	1.
2.	2

Comments :	Record Number:

NOTARY RECORD

Printed Name and Address of Signer:	**Phone Number:**	**Thumb Print:**
	Email:	
	Signer's Signature:	

Service Performed: ☐ Oath ☐ Acknowledgment ☐ Jurat ☐ Other:	**Identification:** ☐ I.D Card ☐ Credible Witness ☐ Drivers License ☐ Known Personally ☐ Passport ☐ Other:	**I.D. Number:** **Issued By:** **Issued Date:**	**Expiration Date:**
Document Type:	**Date/Time Notarized:** AM PM	**Document Date:**	**Fee Charged:**

Printed Name and Address of Witness: **1.** **2.**	**Witness' Signature:** **1.** **2.**
Comments :	**Record Number:**

NOTARY RECORD

Printed Name and Address of Signer:	**Phone Number:**	**Thumb Print:**
	Email:	
	Signer's Signature:	

Service Performed: ☐ Oath ☐ Acknowledgment ☐ Jurat ☐ Other:	**Identification:** ☐ I.D Card ☐ Credible Witness ☐ Drivers License ☐ Known Personally ☐ Passport ☐ Other:	**I.D. Number:** **Issued By:** **Issued Date:**	**Expiration Date:**
Document Type:	**Date/Time Notarized:** AM PM	**Document Date:**	**Fee Charged:**

Printed Name and Address of Witness: **1.** **2.**	**Witness' Signature:** **1.** **2**
Comments :	**Record Number:**

NOTARY RECORD

Printed Name and Address of Signer:	**Phone Number:**	**Thumb Print:**
	Email:	
	Signer's Signature:	

Service Performed: ☐ Oath ☐ Acknowledgment ☐ Jurat ☐ Other:	**Identification:** ☐ I.D Card ☐ Credible Witness ☐ Drivers License ☐ Known Personally ☐ Passport ☐ Other:	**I.D. Number:**	
		Issued By:	
		Issued Date:	**Expiration Date:**
Document Type:	**Date/Time Notarized:** AM PM	**Document Date:**	**Fee Charged:**

Printed Name and Address of Witness: **1.** **2.**	**Witness' Signature:** **1.** **2.**

Comments :	**Record Number:**

NOTARY RECORD

Printed Name and Address of Signer:	**Phone Number:**	**Thumb Print:**
	Email:	
	Signer's Signature:	

Service Performed: ☐ Oath ☐ Acknowledgment ☐ Jurat ☐ Other:	**Identification:** ☐ I.D Card ☐ Credible Witness ☐ Drivers License ☐ Known Personally ☐ Passport ☐ Other:	**I.D. Number:**	
		Issued By:	
		Issued Date:	**Expiration Date:**
Document Type:	**Date/Time Notarized:** AM PM	**Document Date:**	**Fee Charged:**

Printed Name and Address of Witness: **1.** **2.**	**Witness' Signature:** **1.** **2**

Comments :	**Record Number:**

NOTARY RECORD

Printed Name and Address of Signer:	**Phone Number:**	**Thumb Print:**
	Email:	
	Signer's Signature:	

Service Performed: ☐ Oath ☐ Acknowledgment ☐ Jurat ☐ Other:	**Identification:** ☐ I.D Card ☐ Credible Witness ☐ Drivers License ☐ Known Personally ☐ Passport ☐ Other:	**I.D. Number:**	
		Issued By:	
		Issued Date:	**Expiration Date:**
Document Type:	**Date/Time Notarized:** **AM** **PM**	**Document Date:**	**Fee Charged:**

Printed Name and Address of Witness: **1.** **2.**	**Witness' Signature:** **1.** **2.**
Comments :	**Record Number:**

NOTARY RECORD

Printed Name and Address of Signer:	**Phone Number:**	**Thumb Print:**
	Email:	
	Signer's Signature:	

Service Performed: ☐ Oath ☐ Acknowledgment ☐ Jurat ☐ Other:	**Identification:** ☐ I.D Card ☐ Credible Witness ☐ Drivers License ☐ Known Personally ☐ Passport ☐ Other:	**I.D. Number:**	
		Issued By:	
		Issued Date:	**Expiration Date:**
Document Type:	**Date/Time Notarized:** **AM** **PM**	**Document Date:**	**Fee Charged:**

Printed Name and Address of Witness: **1.** **2.**	**Witness' Signature:** **1.** **2**
Comments :	**Record Number:**

NOTARY RECORD

Printed Name and Address of Signer:	Phone Number:	Thumb Print:
	Email:	
	Signer's Signature:	

Service Performed:	Identification:		I.D. Number:	
☐ Oath	☐ I.D Card	☐ Credible Witness	Issued By:	
☐ Acknowledgment	☐ Drivers License	☐ Known Personally		
☐ Jurat	☐ Passport		Issued Date:	Expiration Date:
☐ Other:	☐ Other:			
Document Type:	Date/Time Notarized: AM PM		Document Date:	Fee Charged:

Printed Name and Address of Witness:	Witness' Signature:
1.	1.
2.	2.

Comments :	Record Number:

NOTARY RECORD

Printed Name and Address of Signer:	Phone Number:	Thumb Print:
	Email:	
	Signer's Signature:	

Service Performed:	Identification:		I.D. Number:	
☐ Oath	☐ I.D Card	☐ Credible Witness	Issued By:	
☐ Acknowledgment	☐ Drivers License	☐ Known Personally		
☐ Jurat	☐ Passport		Issued Date:	Expiration Date:
☐ Other:	☐ Other:			
Document Type:	Date/Time Notarized: AM PM		Document Date:	Fee Charged:

Printed Name and Address of Witness:	Witness' Signature:
1.	1.
2.	2

Comments :	Record Number:

NOTARY RECORD

Printed Name and Address of Signer:	Phone Number:	Thumb Print:
	Email:	
	Signer's Signature:	

Service Performed:
- ☐ Oath
- ☐ Acknowledgment
- ☐ Jurat
- ☐ Other:

Identification:
- ☐ I.D Card
- ☐ Credible Witness
- ☐ Drivers License
- ☐ Known Personally
- ☐ Passport
- ☐ Other:

I.D. Number:	
Issued By:	
Issued Date:	Expiration Date:

Document Type:	Date/Time Notarized: AM PM	Document Date:	Fee Charged:

Printed Name and Address of Witness:	Witness' Signature:
1.	1.
2.	2.

Comments :	Record Number:

NOTARY RECORD

Printed Name and Address of Signer:	Phone Number:	Thumb Print:
	Email:	
	Signer's Signature:	

Service Performed:
- ☐ Oath
- ☐ Acknowledgment
- ☐ Jurat
- ☐ Other:

Identification:
- ☐ I.D Card
- ☐ Credible Witness
- ☐ Drivers License
- ☐ Known Personally
- ☐ Passport
- ☐ Other:

I.D. Number:	
Issued By:	
Issued Date:	Expiration Date:

Document Type:	Date/Time Notarized: AM PM	Document Date:	Fee Charged:

Printed Name and Address of Witness:	Witness' Signature:
1.	1.
2.	2

Comments :	Record Number:

NOTARY RECORD

Printed Name and Address of Signer:	Phone Number:	Thumb Print:
	Email:	
	Signer's Signature:	

Service Performed:	Identification:		I.D. Number:	
☐ Oath	☐ I.D Card	☐ Credible Witness	Issued By:	
☐ Acknowledgment	☐ Drivers License	☐ Known Personally		
☐ Jurat	☐ Passport		Issued Date:	Expiration Date:
☐ Other:	☐ Other:			
Document Type:	Date/Time Notarized: AM PM		Document Date:	Fee Charged:

Printed Name and Address of Witness:	Witness' Signature:
1.	1.
2.	2.

Comments :	Record Number:

NOTARY RECORD

Printed Name and Address of Signer:	Phone Number:	Thumb Print:
	Email:	
	Signer's Signature:	

Service Performed:	Identification:		I.D. Number:	
☐ Oath	☐ I.D Card	☐ Credible Witness	Issued By:	
☐ Acknowledgment	☐ Drivers License	☐ Known Personally		
☐ Jurat	☐ Passport		Issued Date:	Expiration Date:
☐ Other:	☐ Other:			
Document Type:	Date/Time Notarized: AM PM		Document Date:	Fee Charged:

Printed Name and Address of Witness:	Witness' Signature:
1.	1.
2.	2

Comments :	Record Number:

NOTARY RECORD

Printed Name and Address of Signer:

Phone Number:

Email:

Signer's Signature:

Thumb Print:

Service Performed:

- ☐ Oath
- ☐ Acknowledgment
- ☐ Jurat
- ☐ Other:

Identification:

- ☐ I.D Card
- ☐ Credible Witness
- ☐ Drivers License
- ☐ Known Personally
- ☐ Passport
- ☐ Other:

I.D. Number:

Issued By:

Issued Date:

Expiration Date:

Document Type:

Date/Time Notarized: **AM** **PM**

Document Date:

Fee Charged:

Printed Name and Address of Witness:

1.

2.

Witness' Signature:

1.

2.

Comments :

Record Number:

NOTARY RECORD

Printed Name and Address of Signer:

Phone Number:

Email:

Signer's Signature:

Thumb Print:

Service Performed:

- ☐ Oath
- ☐ Acknowledgment
- ☐ Jurat
- ☐ Other:

Identification:

- ☐ I.D Card
- ☐ Credible Witness
- ☐ Drivers License
- ☐ Known Personally
- ☐ Passport
- ☐ Other:

I.D. Number:

Issued By:

Issued Date:

Expiration Date:

Document Type:

Date/Time Notarized: **AM** **PM**

Document Date:

Fee Charged:

Printed Name and Address of Witness:

1.

2.

Witness' Signature:

1.

2

Comments :

Record Number:

NOTARY RECORD

Printed Name and Address of Signer:	**Phone Number:**	**Thumb Print:**
	Email:	
	Signer's Signature:	

Service Performed: ☐ Oath ☐ Acknowledgment ☐ Jurat ☐ Other:	**Identification:** ☐ I.D Card ☐ Credible Witness ☐ Drivers License ☐ Known Personally ☐ Passport ☐ Other:	**I.D. Number:**	
		Issued By:	
		Issued Date:	**Expiration Date:**
Document Type:	**Date/Time Notarized:** AM PM	**Document Date:**	**Fee Charged:**

Printed Name and Address of Witness: **1.** **2.**	**Witness' Signature:** **1.** **2.**

Comments :	**Record Number:**

NOTARY RECORD

Printed Name and Address of Signer:	**Phone Number:**	**Thumb Print:**
	Email:	
	Signer's Signature:	

Service Performed: ☐ Oath ☐ Acknowledgment ☐ Jurat ☐ Other:	**Identification:** ☐ I.D Card ☐ Credible Witness ☐ Drivers License ☐ Known Personally ☐ Passport ☐ Other:	**I.D. Number:**	
		Issued By:	
		Issued Date:	**Expiration Date:**
Document Type:	**Date/Time Notarized:** AM PM	**Document Date:**	**Fee Charged:**

Printed Name and Address of Witness: **1.** **2.**	**Witness' Signature:** **1.** **2**

Comments :	**Record Number:**

NOTARY RECORD

Printed Name and Address of Signer:	**Phone Number:**	**Thumb Print:**
	Email:	
	Signer's Signature:	

Service Performed: ☐ Oath ☐ Acknowledgment ☐ Jurat ☐ Other:	**Identification:** ☐ I.D Card ☐ Credible Witness ☐ Drivers License ☐ Known Personally ☐ Passport ☐ Other:	**I.D. Number:**	
		Issued By:	
		Issued Date:	**Expiration Date:**
Document Type:	**Date/Time Notarized:** **AM** **PM**	**Document Date:**	**Fee Charged:**

Printed Name and Address of Witness: **1.** **2.**	**Witness' Signature:** **1.** **2.**
Comments :	**Record Number:**

NOTARY RECORD

Printed Name and Address of Signer:	**Phone Number:**	**Thumb Print:**
	Email:	
	Signer's Signature:	

Service Performed: ☐ Oath ☐ Acknowledgment ☐ Jurat ☐ Other:	**Identification:** ☐ I.D Card ☐ Credible Witness ☐ Drivers License ☐ Known Personally ☐ Passport ☐ Other:	**I.D. Number:**	
		Issued By:	
		Issued Date:	**Expiration Date:**
Document Type:	**Date/Time Notarized:** **AM** **PM**	**Document Date:**	**Fee Charged:**

Printed Name and Address of Witness: **1.** **2.**	**Witness' Signature:** **1.** **2**
Comments :	**Record Number:**

NOTARY RECORD

Printed Name and Address of Signer:	**Phone Number:**	**Thumb Print:**
	Email:	
	Signer's Signature:	

Service Performed: ☐ Oath ☐ Acknowledgment ☐ Jurat ☐ Other:	**Identification:** ☐ I.D Card ☐ Credible Witness ☐ Drivers License ☐ Known Personally ☐ Passport ☐ Other:	**I.D. Number:**	
		Issued By:	
		Issued Date:	**Expiration Date:**
Document Type:	**Date/Time Notarized:** AM PM	**Document Date:**	**Fee Charged:**

Printed Name and Address of Witness: **1.** **2.**	**Witness' Signature:** **1.** **2.**
Comments :	**Record Number:**

NOTARY RECORD

Printed Name and Address of Signer:	**Phone Number:**	**Thumb Print:**
	Email:	
	Signer's Signature:	

Service Performed: ☐ Oath ☐ Acknowledgment ☐ Jurat ☐ Other:	**Identification:** ☐ I.D Card ☐ Credible Witness ☐ Drivers License ☐ Known Personally ☐ Passport ☐ Other:	**I.D. Number:**	
		Issued By:	
		Issued Date:	**Expiration Date:**
Document Type:	**Date/Time Notarized:** AM PM	**Document Date:**	**Fee Charged:**

Printed Name and Address of Witness: **1.** **2.**	**Witness' Signature:** **1.** **2**
Comments :	**Record Number:**

NOTARY RECORD

Printed Name and Address of Signer:	Phone Number:	Thumb Print:
	Email:	
	Signer's Signature:	

Service Performed:	Identification:		I.D. Number:	
☐ Oath	☐ I.D Card	☐ Credible Witness	Issued By:	
☐ Acknowledgment	☐ Drivers License	☐ Known Personally	Issued Date:	Expiration Date:
☐ Jurat	☐ Passport			
☐ Other:	☐ Other:			
Document Type:	Date/Time Notarized: AM PM		Document Date:	Fee Charged:

Printed Name and Address of Witness:	Witness' Signature:
1.	1.
2.	2.

Comments :	Record Number:

NOTARY RECORD

Printed Name and Address of Signer:	Phone Number:	Thumb Print:
	Email:	
	Signer's Signature:	

Service Performed:	Identification:		I.D. Number:	
☐ Oath	☐ I.D Card	☐ Credible Witness	Issued By:	
☐ Acknowledgment	☐ Drivers License	☐ Known Personally	Issued Date:	Expiration Date:
☐ Jurat	☐ Passport			
☐ Other:	☐ Other:			
Document Type:	Date/Time Notarized: AM PM		Document Date:	Fee Charged:

Printed Name and Address of Witness:	Witness' Signature:
1.	1.
2.	2

Comments :	Record Number:

NOTARY RECORD

Printed Name and Address of Signer:	**Phone Number:**	**Thumb Print:**
	Email:	
	Signer's Signature:	

Service Performed: ☐ Oath ☐ Acknowledgment ☐ Jurat ☐ Other:	**Identification:** ☐ I.D Card ☐ Credible Witness ☐ Drivers License ☐ Known Personally ☐ Passport ☐ Other:	**I.D. Number:**	
		Issued By:	
		Issued Date:	**Expiration Date:**
Document Type:	**Date/Time Notarized:** AM PM	**Document Date:**	**Fee Charged:**

Printed Name and Address of Witness: **1.** **2.**	**Witness' Signature:** **1.** **2.**
Comments :	**Record Number:**

NOTARY RECORD

Printed Name and Address of Signer:	**Phone Number:**	**Thumb Print:**
	Email:	
	Signer's Signature:	

Service Performed: ☐ Oath ☐ Acknowledgment ☐ Jurat ☐ Other:	**Identification:** ☐ I.D Card ☐ Credible Witness ☐ Drivers License ☐ Known Personally ☐ Passport ☐ Other:	**I.D. Number:**	
		Issued By:	
		Issued Date:	**Expiration Date:**
Document Type:	**Date/Time Notarized:** AM PM	**Document Date:**	**Fee Charged:**

Printed Name and Address of Witness: **1.** **2.**	**Witness' Signature:** **1.** **2**
Comments :	**Record Number:**

NOTARY RECORD

Printed Name and Address of Signer:	Phone Number:	Thumb Print:
	Email:	
	Signer's Signature:	

Service Performed:	Identification:		I.D. Number:	
☐ Oath	☐ I.D Card	☐ Credible Witness		
☐ Acknowledgment	☐ Drivers License	☐ Known Personally	Issued By:	
☐ Jurat	☐ Passport		Issued Date:	Expiration Date:
☐ Other:	☐ Other:			
Document Type:	Date/Time Notarized: AM PM		Document Date:	Fee Charged:

Printed Name and Address of Witness:	Witness' Signature:
1.	1.
2.	2.

Comments :	Record Number:

NOTARY RECORD

Printed Name and Address of Signer:	Phone Number:	Thumb Print:
	Email:	
	Signer's Signature:	

Service Performed:	Identification:		I.D. Number:	
☐ Oath	☐ I.D Card	☐ Credible Witness		
☐ Acknowledgment	☐ Drivers License	☐ Known Personally	Issued By:	
☐ Jurat	☐ Passport		Issued Date:	Expiration Date:
☐ Other:	☐ Other:			
Document Type:	Date/Time Notarized: AM PM		Document Date:	Fee Charged:

Printed Name and Address of Witness:	Witness' Signature:
1.	1.
2.	2

Comments :	Record Number:

NOTARY RECORD

Printed Name and Address of Signer:	Phone Number:	Thumb Print:
	Email:	
	Signer's Signature:	

Service Performed:	Identification:		I.D. Number:	
☐ Oath	☐ I.D Card	☐ Credible Witness		
☐ Acknowledgment	☐ Drivers License	☐ Known Personally	Issued By:	
☐ Jurat	☐ Passport			
☐ Other:	☐ Other:		Issued Date:	Expiration Date:
Document Type:	Date/Time Notarized: AM PM		Document Date:	Fee Charged:

Printed Name and Address of Witness:	Witness' Signature:
1.	1.
2.	2.

Comments :	Record Number:

NOTARY RECORD

Printed Name and Address of Signer:	Phone Number:	Thumb Print:
	Email:	
	Signer's Signature:	

Service Performed:	Identification:		I.D. Number:	
☐ Oath	☐ I.D Card	☐ Credible Witness		
☐ Acknowledgment	☐ Drivers License	☐ Known Personally	Issued By:	
☐ Jurat	☐ Passport			
☐ Other:	☐ Other:		Issued Date:	Expiration Date:
Document Type:	Date/Time Notarized: AM PM		Document Date:	Fee Charged:

Printed Name and Address of Witness:	Witness' Signature:
1.	1.
2.	2

Comments :	Record Number:

NOTARY RECORD

Printed Name and Address of Signer:	Phone Number:	Thumb Print:
	Email:	
	Signer's Signature:	

Service Performed:	Identification:		I.D. Number:	
☐ Oath	☐ I.D Card	☐ Credible Witness		
☐ Acknowledgment	☐ Drivers License	☐ Known Personally	Issued By:	
☐ Jurat	☐ Passport			
☐ Other:	☐ Other:		Issued Date:	Expiration Date:
Document Type:	Date/Time Notarized: AM PM		Document Date:	Fee Charged:

Printed Name and Address of Witness:	Witness' Signature:
1.	1.
2.	2.

Comments :	Record Number:

NOTARY RECORD

Printed Name and Address of Signer:	Phone Number:	Thumb Print:
	Email:	
	Signer's Signature:	

Service Performed:	Identification:		I.D. Number:	
☐ Oath	☐ I.D Card	☐ Credible Witness		
☐ Acknowledgment	☐ Drivers License	☐ Known Personally	Issued By:	
☐ Jurat	☐ Passport			
☐ Other:	☐ Other:		Issued Date:	Expiration Date:
Document Type:	Date/Time Notarized: AM PM		Document Date:	Fee Charged:

Printed Name and Address of Witness:	Witness' Signature:
1.	1.
2.	2

Comments :	Record Number:

NOTARY RECORD

Printed Name and Address of Signer:	**Phone Number:**	**Thumb Print:**
	Email:	
	Signer's Signature:	

Service Performed: ☐ Oath ☐ Acknowledgment ☐ Jurat ☐ Other:	**Identification:** ☐ I.D Card ☐ Credible Witness ☐ Drivers License ☐ Known Personally ☐ Passport ☐ Other:	**I.D. Number:**	
		Issued By:	
		Issued Date:	**Expiration Date:**
Document Type:	**Date/Time Notarized:** AM PM	**Document Date:**	**Fee Charged:**

Printed Name and Address of Witness: **1.** **2.**	**Witness' Signature:** **1.** **2.**
Comments :	**Record Number:**

NOTARY RECORD

Printed Name and Address of Signer:	**Phone Number:**	**Thumb Print:**
	Email:	
	Signer's Signature:	

Service Performed: ☐ Oath ☐ Acknowledgment ☐ Jurat ☐ Other:	**Identification:** ☐ I.D Card ☐ Credible Witness ☐ Drivers License ☐ Known Personally ☐ Passport ☐ Other:	**I.D. Number:**	
		Issued By:	
		Issued Date:	**Expiration Date:**
Document Type:	**Date/Time Notarized:** AM PM	**Document Date:**	**Fee Charged:**

Printed Name and Address of Witness: **1.** **2.**	**Witness' Signature:** **1.** **2**
Comments :	**Record Number:**

NOTARY RECORD

Printed Name and Address of Signer:	Phone Number:	Thumb Print:
	Email:	
	Signer's Signature:	

Service Performed:	Identification:		I.D. Number:	
☐ Oath	☐ I.D Card	☐ Credible Witness		
☐ Acknowledgment	☐ Drivers License	☐ Known Personally	Issued By:	
☐ Jurat	☐ Passport			
☐ Other:	☐ Other:		Issued Date:	Expiration Date:
Document Type:	Date/Time Notarized:	AM PM	Document Date:	Fee Charged:

Printed Name and Address of Witness:	Witness' Signature:
1.	1.
2.	2.

Comments :	Record Number:

NOTARY RECORD

Printed Name and Address of Signer:	Phone Number:	Thumb Print:
	Email:	
	Signer's Signature:	

Service Performed:	Identification:		I.D. Number:	
☐ Oath	☐ I.D Card	☐ Credible Witness		
☐ Acknowledgment	☐ Drivers License	☐ Known Personally	Issued By:	
☐ Jurat	☐ Passport			
☐ Other:	☐ Other:		Issued Date:	Expiration Date:
Document Type:	Date/Time Notarized:	AM PM	Document Date:	Fee Charged:

Printed Name and Address of Witness:	Witness' Signature:
1.	1.
2.	2

Comments :	Record Number:

NOTARY RECORD

Printed Name and Address of Signer:

Phone Number:

Email:

Signer's Signature:

Thumb Print:

Service Performed:

- ☐ Oath
- ☐ Acknowledgment
- ☐ Jurat
- ☐ Other:

Identification:

- ☐ I.D Card
- ☐ Credible Witness
- ☐ Drivers License
- ☐ Known Personally
- ☐ Passport
- ☐ Other:

I.D. Number:

Issued By:

Issued Date:

Expiration Date:

Document Type:

Date/Time Notarized: AM PM

Document Date:

Fee Charged:

Printed Name and Address of Witness:

1.

2.

Witness' Signature:

1.

2.

Comments :

Record Number:

NOTARY RECORD

Printed Name and Address of Signer:

Phone Number:

Email:

Signer's Signature:

Thumb Print:

Service Performed:

- ☐ Oath
- ☐ Acknowledgment
- ☐ Jurat
- ☐ Other:

Identification:

- ☐ I.D Card
- ☐ Credible Witness
- ☐ Drivers License
- ☐ Known Personally
- ☐ Passport
- ☐ Other:

I.D. Number:

Issued By:

Issued Date:

Expiration Date:

Document Type:

Date/Time Notarized: AM PM

Document Date:

Fee Charged:

Printed Name and Address of Witness:

1.

2.

Witness' Signature:

1.

2

Comments :

Record Number:

NOTARY RECORD

Printed Name and Address of Signer:	**Phone Number:**	**Thumb Print:**
	Email:	
	Signer's Signature:	

Service Performed: ☐ Oath ☐ Acknowledgment ☐ Jurat ☐ Other:	**Identification:** ☐ I.D Card ☐ Credible Witness ☐ Drivers License ☐ Known Personally ☐ Passport ☐ Other:	**I.D. Number:**	
		Issued By:	
		Issued Date:	**Expiration Date:**
Document Type:	**Date/Time Notarized:** AM PM	**Document Date:**	**Fee Charged:**

Printed Name and Address of Witness: 1. 2.	**Witness' Signature:** 1. 2.
Comments :	**Record Number:**

NOTARY RECORD

Printed Name and Address of Signer:	**Phone Number:**	**Thumb Print:**
	Email:	
	Signer's Signature:	

Service Performed: ☐ Oath ☐ Acknowledgment ☐ Jurat ☐ Other:	**Identification:** ☐ I.D Card ☐ Credible Witness ☐ Drivers License ☐ Known Personally ☐ Passport ☐ Other:	**I.D. Number:**	
		Issued By:	
		Issued Date:	**Expiration Date:**
Document Type:	**Date/Time Notarized:** AM PM	**Document Date:**	**Fee Charged:**

Printed Name and Address of Witness: 1. 2.	**Witness' Signature:** 1. 2
Comments :	**Record Number:**

NOTARY RECORD

Printed Name and Address of Signer:

Phone Number:

Email:

Signer's Signature:

Thumb Print:

Service Performed:

- ☐ Oath
- ☐ Acknowledgment
- ☐ Jurat
- ☐ Other:

Identification:

- ☐ I.D Card
- ☐ Credible Witness
- ☐ Drivers License
- ☐ Known Personally
- ☐ Passport
- ☐ Other:

I.D. Number:

Issued By:

Issued Date:

Expiration Date:

Document Type:

Date/Time Notarized: **AM** **PM**

Document Date:

Fee Charged:

Printed Name and Address of Witness:

1.

2.

Witness' Signature:

1.

2.

Comments :

Record Number:

NOTARY RECORD

Printed Name and Address of Signer:

Phone Number:

Email:

Signer's Signature:

Thumb Print:

Service Performed:

- ☐ Oath
- ☐ Acknowledgment
- ☐ Jurat
- ☐ Other:

Identification:

- ☐ I.D Card
- ☐ Credible Witness
- ☐ Drivers License
- ☐ Known Personally
- ☐ Passport
- ☐ Other:

I.D. Number:

Issued By:

Issued Date:

Expiration Date:

Document Type:

Date/Time Notarized: **AM** **PM**

Document Date:

Fee Charged:

Printed Name and Address of Witness:

1.

2.

Witness' Signature:

1.

2

Comments :

Record Number:

NOTARY RECORD

Printed Name and Address of Signer:

Phone Number:

Email:

Signer's Signature:

Thumb Print:

Service Performed:

- ☐ Oath
- ☐ Acknowledgment
- ☐ Jurat
- ☐ Other:

Identification:

- ☐ I.D Card
- ☐ Credible Witness
- ☐ Drivers License
- ☐ Known Personally
- ☐ Passport
- ☐ Other:

I.D. Number:

Issued By:

Issued Date:

Expiration Date:

Document Type:

Date/Time Notarized: **AM** **PM**

Document Date:

Fee Charged:

Printed Name and Address of Witness:

1.

2.

Witness' Signature:

1.

2.

Comments :

Record Number:

NOTARY RECORD

Printed Name and Address of Signer:

Phone Number:

Email:

Signer's Signature:

Thumb Print:

Service Performed:

- ☐ Oath
- ☐ Acknowledgment
- ☐ Jurat
- ☐ Other:

Identification:

- ☐ I.D Card
- ☐ Credible Witness
- ☐ Drivers License
- ☐ Known Personally
- ☐ Passport
- ☐ Other:

I.D. Number:

Issued By:

Issued Date:

Expiration Date:

Document Type:

Date/Time Notarized: **AM** **PM**

Document Date:

Fee Charged:

Printed Name and Address of Witness:

1.

2.

Witness' Signature:

1.

2

Comments :

Record Number:

NOTARY RECORD

Printed Name and Address of Signer:	Phone Number:	Thumb Print:
	Email:	
	Signer's Signature:	

Service Performed:	Identification:		I.D. Number:	
☐ Oath	☐ I.D Card	☐ Credible Witness		
☐ Acknowledgment	☐ Drivers License	☐ Known Personally	Issued By:	
☐ Jurat	☐ Passport			
☐ Other:	☐ Other:		Issued Date:	Expiration Date:
Document Type:	Date/Time Notarized: AM PM		Document Date:	Fee Charged:

Printed Name and Address of Witness:	Witness' Signature:
1.	1.
2.	2.

Comments :	Record Number:

NOTARY RECORD

Printed Name and Address of Signer:	Phone Number:	Thumb Print:
	Email:	
	Signer's Signature:	

Service Performed:	Identification:		I.D. Number:	
☐ Oath	☐ I.D Card	☐ Credible Witness		
☐ Acknowledgment	☐ Drivers License	☐ Known Personally	Issued By:	
☐ Jurat	☐ Passport			
☐ Other:	☐ Other:		Issued Date:	Expiration Date:
Document Type:	Date/Time Notarized: AM PM		Document Date:	Fee Charged:

Printed Name and Address of Witness:	Witness' Signature:
1.	1.
2.	2

Comments :	Record Number:

NOTARY RECORD

Printed Name and Address of Signer:	Phone Number:	Thumb Print:
	Email:	
	Signer's Signature:	

Service Performed:	Identification:		I.D. Number:	
☐ Oath	☐ I.D Card	☐ Credible Witness		
☐ Acknowledgment	☐ Drivers License	☐ Known Personally	Issued By:	
☐ Jurat	☐ Passport			
☐ Other:	☐ Other:		Issued Date:	Expiration Date:
Document Type:	Date/Time Notarized: AM PM		Document Date:	Fee Charged:

Printed Name and Address of Witness:	Witness' Signature:
1.	1.
2.	2.

Comments :	Record Number:

NOTARY RECORD

Printed Name and Address of Signer:	Phone Number:	Thumb Print:
	Email:	
	Signer's Signature:	

Service Performed:	Identification:		I.D. Number:	
☐ Oath	☐ I.D Card	☐ Credible Witness		
☐ Acknowledgment	☐ Drivers License	☐ Known Personally	Issued By:	
☐ Jurat	☐ Passport			
☐ Other:	☐ Other:		Issued Date:	Expiration Date:
Document Type:	Date/Time Notarized: AM PM		Document Date:	Fee Charged:

Printed Name and Address of Witness:	Witness' Signature:
1.	1.
2.	2

Comments :	Record Number:

NOTARY RECORD

Printed Name and Address of Signer:	**Phone Number:**	**Thumb Print:**
	Email:	
	Signer's Signature:	

Service Performed: ☐ Oath ☐ Acknowledgment ☐ Jurat ☐ Other:	**Identification:** ☐ I.D Card ☐ Credible Witness ☐ Drivers License ☐ Known Personally ☐ Passport ☐ Other:	**I.D. Number:**	
		Issued By:	
		Issued Date:	**Expiration Date:**
Document Type:	**Date/Time Notarized:** AM PM	**Document Date:**	**Fee Charged:**

Printed Name and Address of Witness: **1.** **2.**	**Witness' Signature:** **1.** **2.**
Comments :	**Record Number:**

NOTARY RECORD

Printed Name and Address of Signer:	**Phone Number:**	**Thumb Print:**
	Email:	
	Signer's Signature:	

Service Performed: ☐ Oath ☐ Acknowledgment ☐ Jurat ☐ Other:	**Identification:** ☐ I.D Card ☐ Credible Witness ☐ Drivers License ☐ Known Personally ☐ Passport ☐ Other:	**I.D. Number:**	
		Issued By:	
		Issued Date:	**Expiration Date:**
Document Type:	**Date/Time Notarized:** AM PM	**Document Date:**	**Fee Charged:**

Printed Name and Address of Witness: **1.** **2.**	**Witness' Signature:** **1.** **2**
Comments :	**Record Number:**

NOTARY RECORD

Printed Name and Address of Signer:	Phone Number:	Thumb Print:
	Email:	
	Signer's Signature:	

Service Performed:	Identification:		I.D. Number:	
☐ Oath	☐ I.D Card	☐ Credible Witness	Issued By:	
☐ Acknowledgment	☐ Drivers License	☐ Known Personally	Issued Date:	Expiration Date:
☐ Jurat	☐ Passport			
☐ Other:	☐ Other:			
Document Type:	Date/Time Notarized:	AM PM	Document Date:	Fee Charged:

Printed Name and Address of Witness:	Witness' Signature:
1.	1.
2.	2.

Comments :	Record Number:

NOTARY RECORD

Printed Name and Address of Signer:	Phone Number:	Thumb Print:
	Email:	
	Signer's Signature:	

Service Performed:	Identification:		I.D. Number:	
☐ Oath	☐ I.D Card	☐ Credible Witness	Issued By:	
☐ Acknowledgment	☐ Drivers License	☐ Known Personally	Issued Date:	Expiration Date:
☐ Jurat	☐ Passport			
☐ Other:	☐ Other:			
Document Type:	Date/Time Notarized:	AM PM	Document Date:	Fee Charged:

Printed Name and Address of Witness:	Witness' Signature:
1.	1.
2.	2

Comments :	Record Number:

NOTARY RECORD

Printed Name and Address of Signer:

Phone Number:

Email:

Signer's Signature:

Thumb Print:

Service Performed:

- ☐ Oath
- ☐ Acknowledgment
- ☐ Jurat
- ☐ Other:

Identification:

- ☐ I.D Card
- ☐ Credible Witness
- ☐ Drivers License
- ☐ Known Personally
- ☐ Passport
- ☐ Other:

I.D. Number:

Issued By:

Issued Date:

Expiration Date:

Document Type:

Date/Time Notarized: **AM** **PM**

Document Date:

Fee Charged:

Printed Name and Address of Witness:

1.

2.

Witness' Signature:

1.

2.

Comments :

Record Number:

NOTARY RECORD

Printed Name and Address of Signer:

Phone Number:

Email:

Signer's Signature:

Thumb Print:

Service Performed:

- ☐ Oath
- ☐ Acknowledgment
- ☐ Jurat
- ☐ Other:

Identification:

- ☐ I.D Card
- ☐ Credible Witness
- ☐ Drivers License
- ☐ Known Personally
- ☐ Passport
- ☐ Other:

I.D. Number:

Issued By:

Issued Date:

Expiration Date:

Document Type:

Date/Time Notarized: **AM** **PM**

Document Date:

Fee Charged:

Printed Name and Address of Witness:

1.

2.

Witness' Signature:

1.

2

Comments :

Record Number:

NOTARY RECORD

Printed Name and Address of Signer:	**Phone Number:**	**Thumb Print:**
	Email:	
	Signer's Signature:	

Service Performed: ☐ Oath ☐ Acknowledgment ☐ Jurat ☐ Other:	**Identification:** ☐ I.D Card ☐ Credible Witness ☐ Drivers License ☐ Known Personally ☐ Passport ☐ Other:	**I.D. Number:**	
		Issued By:	
		Issued Date:	**Expiration Date:**
Document Type:	**Date/Time Notarized:** AM PM	**Document Date:**	**Fee Charged:**

Printed Name and Address of Witness:	**Witness' Signature:**
1.	**1.**
2.	**2.**

Comments :	**Record Number:**

NOTARY RECORD

Printed Name and Address of Signer:	**Phone Number:**	**Thumb Print:**
	Email:	
	Signer's Signature:	

Service Performed: ☐ Oath ☐ Acknowledgment ☐ Jurat ☐ Other:	**Identification:** ☐ I.D Card ☐ Credible Witness ☐ Drivers License ☐ Known Personally ☐ Passport ☐ Other:	**I.D. Number:**	
		Issued By:	
		Issued Date:	**Expiration Date:**
Document Type:	**Date/Time Notarized:** AM PM	**Document Date:**	**Fee Charged:**

Printed Name and Address of Witness:	**Witness' Signature:**
1.	**1.**
2.	**2**

Comments :	**Record Number:**

NOTARY RECORD

Printed Name and Address of Signer:	Phone Number:	Thumb Print:
	Email:	
	Signer's Signature:	

Service Performed:	Identification:		I.D. Number:	
☐ Oath	☐ I.D Card	☐ Credible Witness		
☐ Acknowledgment	☐ Drivers License	☐ Known Personally	Issued By:	
☐ Jurat	☐ Passport			
☐ Other:	☐ Other:		Issued Date:	Expiration Date:
Document Type:	Date/Time Notarized: AM PM		Document Date:	Fee Charged:

Printed Name and Address of Witness:	Witness' Signature:
1.	1.
2.	2.

Comments :	Record Number:

NOTARY RECORD

Printed Name and Address of Signer:	Phone Number:	Thumb Print:
	Email:	
	Signer's Signature:	

Service Performed:	Identification:		I.D. Number:	
☐ Oath	☐ I.D Card	☐ Credible Witness		
☐ Acknowledgment	☐ Drivers License	☐ Known Personally	Issued By:	
☐ Jurat	☐ Passport			
☐ Other:	☐ Other:		Issued Date:	Expiration Date:
Document Type:	Date/Time Notarized: AM PM		Document Date:	Fee Charged:

Printed Name and Address of Witness:	Witness' Signature:
1.	1.
2.	2

Comments :	Record Number:

NOTARY RECORD

Printed Name and Address of Signer:	**Phone Number:**	**Thumb Print:**
	Email:	
	Signer's Signature:	

Service Performed: ☐ Oath ☐ Acknowledgment ☐ Jurat ☐ Other:	**Identification:** ☐ I.D Card ☐ Credible Witness ☐ Drivers License ☐ Known Personally ☐ Passport ☐ Other:	**I.D. Number:**	
		Issued By:	
		Issued Date:	**Expiration Date:**
Document Type:	**Date/Time Notarized:** **AM PM**	**Document Date:**	**Fee Charged:**

Printed Name and Address of Witness:	**Witness' Signature:**
1.	**1.**
2.	**2.**

Comments :	**Record Number:**

NOTARY RECORD

Printed Name and Address of Signer:	**Phone Number:**	**Thumb Print:**
	Email:	
	Signer's Signature:	

Service Performed: ☐ Oath ☐ Acknowledgment ☐ Jurat ☐ Other:	**Identification:** ☐ I.D Card ☐ Credible Witness ☐ Drivers License ☐ Known Personally ☐ Passport ☐ Other:	**I.D. Number:**	
		Issued By:	
		Issued Date:	**Expiration Date:**
Document Type:	**Date/Time Notarized:** **AM PM**	**Document Date:**	**Fee Charged:**

Printed Name and Address of Witness:	**Witness' Signature:**
1.	**1.**
2.	**2**

Comments :	**Record Number:**

NOTARY RECORD

Printed Name and Address of Signer:	Phone Number:	Thumb Print:
	Email:	
	Signer's Signature:	

Service Performed:	Identification:		I.D. Number:	
☐ Oath	☐ I.D Card	☐ Credible Witness		
☐ Acknowledgment	☐ Drivers License	☐ Known Personally	Issued By:	
☐ Jurat	☐ Passport			
☐ Other:	☐ Other:		Issued Date:	Expiration Date:
Document Type:	Date/Time Notarized:	AM PM	Document Date:	Fee Charged:

Printed Name and Address of Witness:	Witness' Signature:
1.	1.
2.	2.

Comments :	Record Number:

NOTARY RECORD

Printed Name and Address of Signer:	Phone Number:	Thumb Print:
	Email:	
	Signer's Signature:	

Service Performed:	Identification:		I.D. Number:	
☐ Oath	☐ I.D Card	☐ Credible Witness		
☐ Acknowledgment	☐ Drivers License	☐ Known Personally	Issued By:	
☐ Jurat	☐ Passport			
☐ Other:	☐ Other:		Issued Date:	Expiration Date:
Document Type:	Date/Time Notarized:	AM PM	Document Date:	Fee Charged:

Printed Name and Address of Witness:	Witness' Signature:
1.	1.
2.	2

Comments :	Record Number:

NOTARY RECORD

Printed Name and Address of Signer:

Phone Number:

Email:

Signer's Signature:

Thumb Print:

Service Performed:

- ☐ Oath
- ☐ Acknowledgment
- ☐ Jurat
- ☐ Other:

Identification:

- ☐ I.D Card
- ☐ Credible Witness
- ☐ Drivers License
- ☐ Known Personally
- ☐ Passport
- ☐ Other:

I.D. Number:

Issued By:

Issued Date:

Expiration Date:

Document Type:

Date/Time Notarized: **AM** **PM**

Document Date:

Fee Charged:

Printed Name and Address of Witness:

1.

2.

Witness' Signature:

1.

2.

Comments :

Record Number:

NOTARY RECORD

Printed Name and Address of Signer:

Phone Number:

Email:

Signer's Signature:

Thumb Print:

Service Performed:

- ☐ Oath
- ☐ Acknowledgment
- ☐ Jurat
- ☐ Other:

Identification:

- ☐ I.D Card
- ☐ Credible Witness
- ☐ Drivers License
- ☐ Known Personally
- ☐ Passport
- ☐ Other:

I.D. Number:

Issued By:

Issued Date:

Expiration Date:

Document Type:

Date/Time Notarized: **AM** **PM**

Document Date:

Fee Charged:

Printed Name and Address of Witness:

1.

2.

Witness' Signature:

1.

2

Comments :

Record Number:

NOTARY RECORD

Printed Name and Address of Signer:	**Phone Number:**	**Thumb Print:**
	Email:	
	Signer's Signature:	

Service Performed: ☐ Oath ☐ Acknowledgment ☐ Jurat ☐ Other:	**Identification:** ☐ I.D Card ☐ Credible Witness ☐ Drivers License ☐ Known Personally ☐ Passport ☐ Other:	**I.D. Number:**	
		Issued By:	
		Issued Date:	**Expiration Date:**
Document Type:	**Date/Time Notarized:** AM PM	**Document Date:**	**Fee Charged:**

Printed Name and Address of Witness: **1.** **2.**	**Witness' Signature:** **1.** **2.**
Comments :	**Record Number:**

NOTARY RECORD

Printed Name and Address of Signer:	**Phone Number:**	**Thumb Print:**
	Email:	
	Signer's Signature:	

Service Performed: ☐ Oath ☐ Acknowledgment ☐ Jurat ☐ Other:	**Identification:** ☐ I.D Card ☐ Credible Witness ☐ Drivers License ☐ Known Personally ☐ Passport ☐ Other:	**I.D. Number:**	
		Issued By:	
		Issued Date:	**Expiration Date:**
Document Type:	**Date/Time Notarized:** AM PM	**Document Date:**	**Fee Charged:**

Printed Name and Address of Witness: **1.** **2.**	**Witness' Signature:** **1.** **2**
Comments :	**Record Number:**

NOTARY RECORD

Printed Name and Address of Signer:	**Phone Number:**	**Thumb Print:**
	Email:	
	Signer's Signature:	

Service Performed: ☐ Oath ☐ Acknowledgment ☐ Jurat ☐ Other:	**Identification:** ☐ I.D Card ☐ Credible Witness ☐ Drivers License ☐ Known Personally ☐ Passport ☐ Other:	**I.D. Number:** **Issued By:**	
		Issued Date:	**Expiration Date:**
Document Type:	**Date/Time Notarized:** **AM** **PM**	**Document Date:**	**Fee Charged:**

Printed Name and Address of Witness: **1.** **2.**	**Witness' Signature:** **1.** **2.**
Comments :	**Record Number:**

NOTARY RECORD

Printed Name and Address of Signer:	**Phone Number:**	**Thumb Print:**
	Email:	
	Signer's Signature:	

Service Performed: ☐ Oath ☐ Acknowledgment ☐ Jurat ☐ Other:	**Identification:** ☐ I.D Card ☐ Credible Witness ☐ Drivers License ☐ Known Personally ☐ Passport ☐ Other:	**I.D. Number:** **Issued By:**	
		Issued Date:	**Expiration Date:**
Document Type:	**Date/Time Notarized:** **AM** **PM**	**Document Date:**	**Fee Charged:**

Printed Name and Address of Witness: **1.** **2.**	**Witness' Signature:** **1.** **2**
Comments :	**Record Number:**

NOTARY RECORD

Printed Name and Address of Signer:	Phone Number:	Thumb Print:
	Email:	
	Signer's Signature:	

Service Performed:	Identification:		I.D. Number:	
☐ Oath	☐ I.D Card	☐ Credible Witness	Issued By:	
☐ Acknowledgment	☐ Drivers License	☐ Known Personally		
☐ Jurat	☐ Passport		Issued Date:	Expiration Date:
☐ Other:	☐ Other:			
Document Type:	Date/Time Notarized: AM PM		Document Date:	Fee Charged:

Printed Name and Address of Witness:	Witness' Signature:
1.	1.
2.	2.

Comments :	Record Number:

NOTARY RECORD

Printed Name and Address of Signer:	Phone Number:	Thumb Print:
	Email:	
	Signer's Signature:	

Service Performed:	Identification:		I.D. Number:	
☐ Oath	☐ I.D Card	☐ Credible Witness	Issued By:	
☐ Acknowledgment	☐ Drivers License	☐ Known Personally		
☐ Jurat	☐ Passport		Issued Date:	Expiration Date:
☐ Other:	☐ Other:			
Document Type:	Date/Time Notarized: AM PM		Document Date:	Fee Charged:

Printed Name and Address of Witness:	Witness' Signature:
1.	1.
2.	2

Comments :	Record Number:

NOTARY RECORD

Printed Name and Address of Signer:	**Phone Number:**	**Thumb Print:**
	Email:	
	Signer's Signature:	

Service Performed: ☐ Oath ☐ Acknowledgment ☐ Jurat ☐ Other:	**Identification:** ☐ I.D Card ☐ Credible Witness ☐ Drivers License ☐ Known Personally ☐ Passport ☐ Other:	**I.D. Number:**	
		Issued By:	
		Issued Date:	**Expiration Date:**
Document Type:	**Date/Time Notarized:** **AM** **PM**	**Document Date:**	**Fee Charged:**

Printed Name and Address of Witness: **1.** **2.**	**Witness' Signature:** **1.** **2.**

Comments :	**Record Number:**

NOTARY RECORD

Printed Name and Address of Signer:	**Phone Number:**	**Thumb Print:**
	Email:	
	Signer's Signature:	

Service Performed: ☐ Oath ☐ Acknowledgment ☐ Jurat ☐ Other:	**Identification:** ☐ I.D Card ☐ Credible Witness ☐ Drivers License ☐ Known Personally ☐ Passport ☐ Other:	**I.D. Number:**	
		Issued By:	
		Issued Date:	**Expiration Date:**
Document Type:	**Date/Time Notarized:** **AM** **PM**	**Document Date:**	**Fee Charged:**

Printed Name and Address of Witness: **1.** **2.**	**Witness' Signature:** **1.** **2**

Comments :	**Record Number:**

NOTARY RECORD

Printed Name and Address of Signer:	Phone Number:	Thumb Print:
	Email:	
	Signer's Signature:	

Service Performed:	Identification:		I.D. Number:	
☐ Oath	☐ I.D Card	☐ Credible Witness		
☐ Acknowledgment	☐ Drivers License	☐ Known Personally	Issued By:	
☐ Jurat	☐ Passport			
☐ Other:	☐ Other:		Issued Date:	Expiration Date:
Document Type:	Date/Time Notarized:	AM PM	Document Date:	Fee Charged:

Printed Name and Address of Witness:	Witness' Signature:
1.	1.
2.	2.

Comments :	Record Number:

NOTARY RECORD

Printed Name and Address of Signer:	Phone Number:	Thumb Print:
	Email:	
	Signer's Signature:	

Service Performed:	Identification:		I.D. Number:	
☐ Oath	☐ I.D Card	☐ Credible Witness		
☐ Acknowledgment	☐ Drivers License	☐ Known Personally	Issued By:	
☐ Jurat	☐ Passport			
☐ Other:	☐ Other:		Issued Date:	Expiration Date:
Document Type:	Date/Time Notarized:	AM PM	Document Date:	Fee Charged:

Printed Name and Address of Witness:	Witness' Signature:
1.	1.
2.	2

Comments :	Record Number:

NOTARY RECORD

Printed Name and Address of Signer:	**Phone Number:**	**Thumb Print:**
	Email:	
	Signer's Signature:	

Service Performed: ☐ Oath ☐ Acknowledgment ☐ Jurat ☐ Other:	**Identification:** ☐ I.D Card ☐ Credible Witness ☐ Drivers License ☐ Known Personally ☐ Passport ☐ Other:	**I.D. Number:**	
		Issued By:	
		Issued Date:	**Expiration Date:**
Document Type:	**Date/Time Notarized:** **AM** **PM**	**Document Date:**	**Fee Charged:**

Printed Name and Address of Witness: **1.** **2.**	**Witness' Signature:** **1.** **2.**

Comments :	**Record Number:**

NOTARY RECORD

Printed Name and Address of Signer:	**Phone Number:**	**Thumb Print:**
	Email:	
	Signer's Signature:	

Service Performed: ☐ Oath ☐ Acknowledgment ☐ Jurat ☐ Other:	**Identification:** ☐ I.D Card ☐ Credible Witness ☐ Drivers License ☐ Known Personally ☐ Passport ☐ Other:	**I.D. Number:**	
		Issued By:	
		Issued Date:	**Expiration Date:**
Document Type:	**Date/Time Notarized:** **AM** **PM**	**Document Date:**	**Fee Charged:**

Printed Name and Address of Witness: **1.** **2.**	**Witness' Signature:** **1.** **2**

Comments :	**Record Number:**

NOTARY RECORD

Printed Name and Address of Signer:	Phone Number:	Thumb Print:
	Email:	
	Signer's Signature:	

Service Performed:	Identification:		I.D. Number:	
☐ Oath	☐ I.D Card	☐ Credible Witness	Issued By:	
☐ Acknowledgment	☐ Drivers License	☐ Known Personally		
☐ Jurat	☐ Passport		Issued Date:	Expiration Date:
☐ Other:	☐ Other:			
Document Type:	Date/Time Notarized: AM PM		Document Date:	Fee Charged:

Printed Name and Address of Witness:	Witness' Signature:
1.	1.
2.	2.

Comments :	Record Number:

NOTARY RECORD

Printed Name and Address of Signer:	Phone Number:	Thumb Print:
	Email:	
	Signer's Signature:	

Service Performed:	Identification:		I.D. Number:	
☐ Oath	☐ I.D Card	☐ Credible Witness	Issued By:	
☐ Acknowledgment	☐ Drivers License	☐ Known Personally		
☐ Jurat	☐ Passport		Issued Date:	Expiration Date:
☐ Other:	☐ Other:			
Document Type:	Date/Time Notarized: AM PM		Document Date:	Fee Charged:

Printed Name and Address of Witness:	Witness' Signature:
1.	1.
2.	2

Comments :	Record Number:

NOTARY RECORD

Printed Name and Address of Signer:	Phone Number:	Thumb Print:
	Email:	
	Signer's Signature:	

Service Performed:
- ☐ Oath
- ☐ Acknowledgment
- ☐ Jurat
- ☐ Other:

Identification:
- ☐ I.D Card
- ☐ Drivers License
- ☐ Passport
- ☐ Other:
- ☐ Credible Witness
- ☐ Known Personally

I.D. Number:	
Issued By:	
Issued Date:	Expiration Date:

Document Type:	Date/Time Notarized: AM PM	Document Date:	Fee Charged:

Printed Name and Address of Witness:	Witness' Signature:
1.	1.
2.	2.

Comments :	Record Number:

NOTARY RECORD

Printed Name and Address of Signer:	Phone Number:	Thumb Print:
	Email:	
	Signer's Signature:	

Service Performed:
- ☐ Oath
- ☐ Acknowledgment
- ☐ Jurat
- ☐ Other:

Identification:
- ☐ I.D Card
- ☐ Drivers License
- ☐ Passport
- ☐ Other:
- ☐ Credible Witness
- ☐ Known Personally

I.D. Number:	
Issued By:	
Issued Date:	Expiration Date:

Document Type:	Date/Time Notarized: AM PM	Document Date:	Fee Charged:

Printed Name and Address of Witness:	Witness' Signature:
1.	1.
2.	2

Comments :	Record Number:

NOTARY RECORD

Printed Name and Address of Signer:	**Phone Number:**	**Thumb Print:**
	Email:	
	Signer's Signature:	

Service Performed: ☐ Oath ☐ Acknowledgment ☐ Jurat ☐ Other:	**Identification:** ☐ I.D Card ☐ Credible Witness ☐ Drivers License ☐ Known Personally ☐ Passport ☐ Other:	**I.D. Number:**	
		Issued By:	
		Issued Date:	**Expiration Date:**
Document Type:	**Date/Time Notarized:** AM PM	**Document Date:**	**Fee Charged:**

Printed Name and Address of Witness: **1.** **2.**	**Witness' Signature:** **1.** **2.**
Comments :	**Record Number:**

NOTARY RECORD

Printed Name and Address of Signer:	**Phone Number:**	**Thumb Print:**
	Email:	
	Signer's Signature:	

Service Performed: ☐ Oath ☐ Acknowledgment ☐ Jurat ☐ Other:	**Identification:** ☐ I.D Card ☐ Credible Witness ☐ Drivers License ☐ Known Personally ☐ Passport ☐ Other:	**I.D. Number:**	
		Issued By:	
		Issued Date:	**Expiration Date:**
Document Type:	**Date/Time Notarized:** AM PM	**Document Date:**	**Fee Charged:**

Printed Name and Address of Witness: **1.** **2.**	**Witness' Signature:** **1.** **2**
Comments :	**Record Number:**

NOTARY RECORD

Printed Name and Address of Signer:	Phone Number:	Thumb Print:
	Email:	
	Signer's Signature:	

Service Performed:	Identification:		I.D. Number:	
☐ Oath	☐ I.D Card	☐ Credible Witness	Issued By:	
☐ Acknowledgment	☐ Drivers License	☐ Known Personally	Issued Date:	Expiration Date:
☐ Jurat	☐ Passport			
☐ Other:	☐ Other:			
Document Type:	Date/Time Notarized: AM PM		Document Date:	Fee Charged:

Printed Name and Address of Witness:	Witness' Signature:
1.	1.
2.	2.

Comments :	Record Number:

NOTARY RECORD

Printed Name and Address of Signer:	Phone Number:	Thumb Print:
	Email:	
	Signer's Signature:	

Service Performed:	Identification:		I.D. Number:	
☐ Oath	☐ I.D Card	☐ Credible Witness	Issued By:	
☐ Acknowledgment	☐ Drivers License	☐ Known Personally	Issued Date:	Expiration Date:
☐ Jurat	☐ Passport			
☐ Other:	☐ Other:			
Document Type:	Date/Time Notarized: AM PM		Document Date:	Fee Charged:

Printed Name and Address of Witness:	Witness' Signature:
1.	1.
2.	2

Comments :	Record Number:

NOTARY RECORD

Printed Name and Address of Signer:	Phone Number:	Thumb Print:
	Email:	
	Signer's Signature:	

Service Performed:	Identification:		I.D. Number:	
☐ Oath	☐ I.D Card	☐ Credible Witness		
☐ Acknowledgment	☐ Drivers License	☐ Known Personally	Issued By:	
☐ Jurat	☐ Passport			
☐ Other:	☐ Other:		Issued Date:	Expiration Date:
Document Type:	Date/Time Notarized:	AM PM	Document Date:	Fee Charged:

Printed Name and Address of Witness:	Witness' Signature:
1.	1.
2.	2.

Comments :	Record Number:

NOTARY RECORD

Printed Name and Address of Signer:	Phone Number:	Thumb Print:
	Email:	
	Signer's Signature:	

Service Performed:	Identification:		I.D. Number:	
☐ Oath	☐ I.D Card	☐ Credible Witness		
☐ Acknowledgment	☐ Drivers License	☐ Known Personally	Issued By:	
☐ Jurat	☐ Passport			
☐ Other:	☐ Other:		Issued Date:	Expiration Date:
Document Type:	Date/Time Notarized:	AM PM	Document Date:	Fee Charged:

Printed Name and Address of Witness:	Witness' Signature:
1.	1.
2.	2

Comments :	Record Number:

NOTARY RECORD

Printed Name and Address of Signer:	Phone Number:	Thumb Print:
	Email:	
	Signer's Signature:	

Service Performed:	Identification:		I.D. Number:
☐ Oath	☐ I.D Card	☐ Credible Witness	Issued By:
☐ Acknowledgment	☐ Drivers License	☐ Known Personally	
☐ Jurat	☐ Passport		Issued Date: / Expiration Date:
☐ Other:	☐ Other:		

Document Type:	Date/Time Notarized: AM PM	Document Date:	Fee Charged:

Printed Name and Address of Witness:	Witness' Signature:
1.	1.
2.	2.

Comments :	Record Number:

NOTARY RECORD

Printed Name and Address of Signer:	Phone Number:	Thumb Print:
	Email:	
	Signer's Signature:	

Service Performed:	Identification:		I.D. Number:
☐ Oath	☐ I.D Card	☐ Credible Witness	Issued By:
☐ Acknowledgment	☐ Drivers License	☐ Known Personally	
☐ Jurat	☐ Passport		Issued Date: / Expiration Date:
☐ Other:	☐ Other:		

Document Type:	Date/Time Notarized: AM PM	Document Date:	Fee Charged:

Printed Name and Address of Witness:	Witness' Signature:
1.	1.
2.	2

Comments :	Record Number:

NOTARY RECORD

Printed Name and Address of Signer:	Phone Number:	Thumb Print:
	Email:	
	Signer's Signature:	

Service Performed:	Identification:		I.D. Number:	
☐ Oath	☐ I.D Card	☐ Credible Witness		
☐ Acknowledgment	☐ Drivers License	☐ Known Personally	Issued By:	
☐ Jurat	☐ Passport			
☐ Other:	☐ Other:		Issued Date:	Expiration Date:
Document Type:	Date/Time Notarized: AM PM		Document Date:	Fee Charged:

Printed Name and Address of Witness:	Witness' Signature:
1.	1.
2.	2.

Comments :	Record Number:

NOTARY RECORD

Printed Name and Address of Signer:	Phone Number:	Thumb Print:
	Email:	
	Signer's Signature:	

Service Performed:	Identification:		I.D. Number:	
☐ Oath	☐ I.D Card	☐ Credible Witness		
☐ Acknowledgment	☐ Drivers License	☐ Known Personally	Issued By:	
☐ Jurat	☐ Passport			
☐ Other:	☐ Other:		Issued Date:	Expiration Date:
Document Type:	Date/Time Notarized: AM PM		Document Date:	Fee Charged:

Printed Name and Address of Witness:	Witness' Signature:
1.	1.
2.	2

Comments :	Record Number:

NOTARY RECORD

Printed Name and Address of Signer:	Phone Number:	Thumb Print:
	Email:	
	Signer's Signature:	

Service Performed:	Identification:		I.D. Number:	
☐ Oath	☐ I.D Card	☐ Credible Witness		
☐ Acknowledgment	☐ Drivers License	☐ Known Personally	Issued By:	
☐ Jurat	☐ Passport			
☐ Other:	☐ Other:		Issued Date:	Expiration Date:
Document Type:	Date/Time Notarized: AM PM		Document Date:	Fee Charged:

Printed Name and Address of Witness:	Witness' Signature:
1.	1.
2.	2.

Comments :	Record Number:

NOTARY RECORD

Printed Name and Address of Signer:	Phone Number:	Thumb Print:
	Email:	
	Signer's Signature:	

Service Performed:	Identification:		I.D. Number:	
☐ Oath	☐ I.D Card	☐ Credible Witness		
☐ Acknowledgment	☐ Drivers License	☐ Known Personally	Issued By:	
☐ Jurat	☐ Passport			
☐ Other:	☐ Other:		Issued Date:	Expiration Date:
Document Type:	Date/Time Notarized: AM PM		Document Date:	Fee Charged:

Printed Name and Address of Witness:	Witness' Signature:
1.	1.
2.	2

Comments :	Record Number:

NOTARY RECORD

Printed Name and Address of Signer:	Phone Number:	Thumb Print:
	Email:	
	Signer's Signature:	

Service Performed:	Identification:		I.D. Number:	
☐ Oath	☐ I.D Card	☐ Credible Witness	Issued By:	
☐ Acknowledgment	☐ Drivers License	☐ Known Personally	Issued Date:	Expiration Date:
☐ Jurat	☐ Passport			
☐ Other:	☐ Other:			
Document Type:	Date/Time Notarized: AM PM		Document Date:	Fee Charged:

Printed Name and Address of Witness:	Witness' Signature:
1.	1.
2.	2.

Comments :	Record Number:

NOTARY RECORD

Printed Name and Address of Signer:	Phone Number:	Thumb Print:
	Email:	
	Signer's Signature:	

Service Performed:	Identification:		I.D. Number:	
☐ Oath	☐ I.D Card	☐ Credible Witness	Issued By:	
☐ Acknowledgment	☐ Drivers License	☐ Known Personally	Issued Date:	Expiration Date:
☐ Jurat	☐ Passport			
☐ Other:	☐ Other:			
Document Type:	Date/Time Notarized: AM PM		Document Date:	Fee Charged:

Printed Name and Address of Witness:	Witness' Signature:
1.	1.
2.	2

Comments :	Record Number:

NOTARY RECORD

Printed Name and Address of Signer:

Phone Number:

Email:

Signer's Signature:

Thumb Print:

Service Performed:

- ☐ Oath
- ☐ Acknowledgment
- ☐ Jurat
- ☐ Other:

Identification:

- ☐ I.D Card
- ☐ Credible Witness
- ☐ Drivers License
- ☐ Known Personally
- ☐ Passport
- ☐ Other:

I.D. Number:

Issued By:

Issued Date:

Expiration Date:

Document Type:

Date/Time Notarized: **AM** **PM**

Document Date:

Fee Charged:

Printed Name and Address of Witness:

1.

2.

Witness' Signature:

1.

2.

Comments :

Record Number:

NOTARY RECORD

Printed Name and Address of Signer:

Phone Number:

Email:

Signer's Signature:

Thumb Print:

Service Performed:

- ☐ Oath
- ☐ Acknowledgment
- ☐ Jurat
- ☐ Other:

Identification:

- ☐ I.D Card
- ☐ Credible Witness
- ☐ Drivers License
- ☐ Known Personally
- ☐ Passport
- ☐ Other:

I.D. Number:

Issued By:

Issued Date:

Expiration Date:

Document Type:

Date/Time Notarized: **AM** **PM**

Document Date:

Fee Charged:

Printed Name and Address of Witness:

1.

2.

Witness' Signature:

1.

2

Comments :

Record Number:

NOTARY RECORD

Printed Name and Address of Signer:	Phone Number:	Thumb Print:
	Email:	
	Signer's Signature:	

Service Performed:	Identification:		I.D. Number:	
☐ Oath	☐ I.D Card	☐ Credible Witness		
☐ Acknowledgment	☐ Drivers License	☐ Known Personally	Issued By:	
☐ Jurat	☐ Passport			
☐ Other:	☐ Other:		Issued Date:	Expiration Date:
Document Type:	Date/Time Notarized: AM PM		Document Date:	Fee Charged:

Printed Name and Address of Witness:	Witness' Signature:
1.	1.
2.	2.

Comments :	Record Number:

NOTARY RECORD

Printed Name and Address of Signer:	Phone Number:	Thumb Print:
	Email:	
	Signer's Signature:	

Service Performed:	Identification:		I.D. Number:	
☐ Oath	☐ I.D Card	☐ Credible Witness		
☐ Acknowledgment	☐ Drivers License	☐ Known Personally	Issued By:	
☐ Jurat	☐ Passport			
☐ Other:	☐ Other:		Issued Date:	Expiration Date:
Document Type:	Date/Time Notarized: AM PM		Document Date:	Fee Charged:

Printed Name and Address of Witness:	Witness' Signature:
1.	1.
2.	2

Comments :	Record Number:

NOTARY RECORD

Printed Name and Address of Signer:	Phone Number:	Thumb Print:
	Email:	
	Signer's Signature:	

Service Performed:	Identification:		I.D. Number:	
☐ Oath	☐ I.D Card	☐ Credible Witness	Issued By:	
☐ Acknowledgment	☐ Drivers License	☐ Known Personally		
☐ Jurat	☐ Passport		Issued Date:	Expiration Date:
☐ Other:	☐ Other:			
Document Type:	Date/Time Notarized:	AM PM	Document Date:	Fee Charged:

Printed Name and Address of Witness:	Witness' Signature:
1.	1.
2.	2.

Comments :	Record Number:

NOTARY RECORD

Printed Name and Address of Signer:	Phone Number:	Thumb Print:
	Email:	
	Signer's Signature:	

Service Performed:	Identification:		I.D. Number:	
☐ Oath	☐ I.D Card	☐ Credible Witness	Issued By:	
☐ Acknowledgment	☐ Drivers License	☐ Known Personally		
☐ Jurat	☐ Passport		Issued Date:	Expiration Date:
☐ Other:	☐ Other:			
Document Type:	Date/Time Notarized:	AM PM	Document Date:	Fee Charged:

Printed Name and Address of Witness:	Witness' Signature:
1.	1.
2.	2

Comments :	Record Number:

NOTARY RECORD

Printed Name and Address of Signer:	Phone Number:	Thumb Print:
	Email:	
	Signer's Signature:	

Service Performed:	Identification:		I.D. Number:	
☐ Oath	☐ I.D Card	☐ Credible Witness	Issued By:	
☐ Acknowledgment	☐ Drivers License	☐ Known Personally	Issued Date:	Expiration Date:
☐ Jurat	☐ Passport			
☐ Other:	☐ Other:			
Document Type:	Date/Time Notarized: AM PM		Document Date:	Fee Charged:

Printed Name and Address of Witness:	Witness' Signature:
1.	1.
2.	2.

Comments :	Record Number:

NOTARY RECORD

Printed Name and Address of Signer:	Phone Number:	Thumb Print:
	Email:	
	Signer's Signature:	

Service Performed:	Identification:		I.D. Number:	
☐ Oath	☐ I.D Card	☐ Credible Witness	Issued By:	
☐ Acknowledgment	☐ Drivers License	☐ Known Personally	Issued Date:	Expiration Date:
☐ Jurat	☐ Passport			
☐ Other:	☐ Other:			
Document Type:	Date/Time Notarized: AM PM		Document Date:	Fee Charged:

Printed Name and Address of Witness:	Witness' Signature:
1.	1.
2.	2

Comments :	Record Number:

NOTARY RECORD

Printed Name and Address of Signer:	Phone Number:	Thumb Print:
	Email:	
	Signer's Signature:	

Service Performed:	Identification:		I.D. Number:	
☐ Oath	☐ I.D Card	☐ Credible Witness	Issued By:	
☐ Acknowledgment	☐ Drivers License	☐ Known Personally	Issued Date:	Expiration Date:
☐ Jurat	☐ Passport			
☐ Other:	☐ Other:			
Document Type:	Date/Time Notarized:	AM PM	Document Date:	Fee Charged:

Printed Name and Address of Witness:	Witness' Signature:
1.	1.
2.	2.

Comments :	Record Number:

NOTARY RECORD

Printed Name and Address of Signer:	Phone Number:	Thumb Print:
	Email:	
	Signer's Signature:	

Service Performed:	Identification:		I.D. Number:	
☐ Oath	☐ I.D Card	☐ Credible Witness	Issued By:	
☐ Acknowledgment	☐ Drivers License	☐ Known Personally	Issued Date:	Expiration Date:
☐ Jurat	☐ Passport			
☐ Other:	☐ Other:			
Document Type:	Date/Time Notarized:	AM PM	Document Date:	Fee Charged:

Printed Name and Address of Witness:	Witness' Signature:
1.	1.
2.	2

Comments :	Record Number:

NOTARY RECORD

Printed Name and Address of Signer:

Phone Number:

Email:

Signer's Signature:

Thumb Print:

Service Performed:
- ☐ Oath
- ☐ Acknowledgment
- ☐ Jurat
- ☐ Other:

Identification:
- ☐ I.D Card
- ☐ Credible Witness
- ☐ Drivers License
- ☐ Known Personally
- ☐ Passport
- ☐ Other:

I.D. Number:

Issued By:

Issued Date:

Expiration Date:

Document Type:

Date/Time Notarized: **AM PM**

Document Date:

Fee Charged:

Printed Name and Address of Witness:

1.

2.

Witness' Signature:

1.

2.

Comments :

Record Number:

NOTARY RECORD

Printed Name and Address of Signer:

Phone Number:

Email:

Signer's Signature:

Thumb Print:

Service Performed:
- ☐ Oath
- ☐ Acknowledgment
- ☐ Jurat
- ☐ Other:

Identification:
- ☐ I.D Card
- ☐ Credible Witness
- ☐ Drivers License
- ☐ Known Personally
- ☐ Passport
- ☐ Other:

I.D. Number:

Issued By:

Issued Date:

Expiration Date:

Document Type:

Date/Time Notarized: **AM PM**

Document Date:

Fee Charged:

Printed Name and Address of Witness:

1.

2.

Witness' Signature:

1.

2

Comments :

Record Number:

NOTARY RECORD

Printed Name and Address of Signer:	Phone Number:	Thumb Print:
	Email:	
	Signer's Signature:	

Service Performed:	Identification:		I.D. Number:	
☐ Oath	☐ I.D Card	☐ Credible Witness		
☐ Acknowledgment	☐ Drivers License	☐ Known Personally	Issued By:	
☐ Jurat	☐ Passport			
☐ Other:	☐ Other:		Issued Date:	Expiration Date:
Document Type:	Date/Time Notarized:	AM PM	Document Date:	Fee Charged:

Printed Name and Address of Witness:	Witness' Signature:
1.	1.
2.	2.

Comments :	Record Number:

NOTARY RECORD

Printed Name and Address of Signer:	Phone Number:	Thumb Print:
	Email:	
	Signer's Signature:	

Service Performed:	Identification:		I.D. Number:	
☐ Oath	☐ I.D Card	☐ Credible Witness		
☐ Acknowledgment	☐ Drivers License	☐ Known Personally	Issued By:	
☐ Jurat	☐ Passport			
☐ Other:	☐ Other:		Issued Date:	Expiration Date:
Document Type:	Date/Time Notarized:	AM PM	Document Date:	Fee Charged:

Printed Name and Address of Witness:	Witness' Signature:
1.	1.
2.	2

Comments :	Record Number:

NOTARY RECORD

Printed Name and Address of Signer:

Phone Number:

Email:

Signer's Signature:

Thumb Print:

Service Performed:

- ☐ Oath
- ☐ Acknowledgment
- ☐ Jurat
- ☐ Other:

Identification:

- ☐ I.D Card
- ☐ Credible Witness
- ☐ Drivers License
- ☐ Known Personally
- ☐ Passport
- ☐ Other:

I.D. Number:

Issued By:

Issued Date:

Expiration Date:

Document Type:

Date/Time Notarized: **AM** **PM**

Document Date:

Fee Charged:

Printed Name and Address of Witness:

1.

2.

Witness' Signature:

1.

2.

Comments :

Record Number:

NOTARY RECORD

Printed Name and Address of Signer:

Phone Number:

Email:

Signer's Signature:

Thumb Print:

Service Performed:

- ☐ Oath
- ☐ Acknowledgment
- ☐ Jurat
- ☐ Other:

Identification:

- ☐ I.D Card
- ☐ Credible Witness
- ☐ Drivers License
- ☐ Known Personally
- ☐ Passport
- ☐ Other:

I.D. Number:

Issued By:

Issued Date:

Expiration Date:

Document Type:

Date/Time Notarized: **AM** **PM**

Document Date:

Fee Charged:

Printed Name and Address of Witness:

1.

2.

Witness' Signature:

1.

2

Comments :

Record Number:

NOTARY RECORD

Printed Name and Address of Signer:	**Phone Number:** **Email:** **Signer's Signature:**	**Thumb Print:**

Service Performed: ☐ Oath ☐ Acknowledgment ☐ Jurat ☐ Other:	**Identification:** ☐ I.D Card ☐ Credible Witness ☐ Drivers License ☐ Known Personally ☐ Passport ☐ Other:	**I.D. Number:** **Issued By:** **Issued Date:**	**Expiration Date:**
Document Type:	**Date/Time Notarized:** AM PM	**Document Date:**	**Fee Charged:**

Printed Name and Address of Witness: **1.** **2.**	**Witness' Signature:** **1.** **2.**
Comments :	**Record Number:**

NOTARY RECORD

Printed Name and Address of Signer:	**Phone Number:** **Email:** **Signer's Signature:**	**Thumb Print:**

Service Performed: ☐ Oath ☐ Acknowledgment ☐ Jurat ☐ Other:	**Identification:** ☐ I.D Card ☐ Credible Witness ☐ Drivers License ☐ Known Personally ☐ Passport ☐ Other:	**I.D. Number:** **Issued By:** **Issued Date:**	**Expiration Date:**
Document Type:	**Date/Time Notarized:** AM PM	**Document Date:**	**Fee Charged:**

Printed Name and Address of Witness: **1.** **2.**	**Witness' Signature:** **1.** **2**
Comments :	**Record Number:**

NOTARY RECORD

Printed Name and Address of Signer:	Phone Number:	Thumb Print:
	Email:	
	Signer's Signature:	

Service Performed:	Identification:		I.D. Number:	
☐ Oath	☐ I.D Card	☐ Credible Witness		
☐ Acknowledgment	☐ Drivers License	☐ Known Personally	Issued By:	
☐ Jurat	☐ Passport			
☐ Other:	☐ Other:		Issued Date:	Expiration Date:
Document Type:	Date/Time Notarized:	AM PM	Document Date:	Fee Charged:

Printed Name and Address of Witness:	Witness' Signature:
1.	1.
2.	2.

Comments :	Record Number:

NOTARY RECORD

Printed Name and Address of Signer:	Phone Number:	Thumb Print:
	Email:	
	Signer's Signature:	

Service Performed:	Identification:		I.D. Number:	
☐ Oath	☐ I.D Card	☐ Credible Witness		
☐ Acknowledgment	☐ Drivers License	☐ Known Personally	Issued By:	
☐ Jurat	☐ Passport			
☐ Other:	☐ Other:		Issued Date:	Expiration Date:
Document Type:	Date/Time Notarized:	AM PM	Document Date:	Fee Charged:

Printed Name and Address of Witness:	Witness' Signature:
1.	1.
2.	2

Comments :	Record Number:

NOTARY RECORD

Printed Name and Address of Signer:

Phone Number:

Email:

Signer's Signature:

Thumb Print:

Service Performed:

- ☐ Oath
- ☐ Acknowledgment
- ☐ Jurat
- ☐ Other:

Identification:

- ☐ I.D Card
- ☐ Credible Witness
- ☐ Drivers License
- ☐ Known Personally
- ☐ Passport
- ☐ Other:

I.D. Number:

Issued By:

Issued Date:

Expiration Date:

Document Type:

Date/Time Notarized: **AM** **PM**

Document Date:

Fee Charged:

Printed Name and Address of Witness:

1.

2.

Witness' Signature:

1.

2.

Comments :

Record Number:

NOTARY RECORD

Printed Name and Address of Signer:

Phone Number:

Email:

Signer's Signature:

Thumb Print:

Service Performed:

- ☐ Oath
- ☐ Acknowledgment
- ☐ Jurat
- ☐ Other:

Identification:

- ☐ I.D Card
- ☐ Credible Witness
- ☐ Drivers License
- ☐ Known Personally
- ☐ Passport
- ☐ Other:

I.D. Number:

Issued By:

Issued Date:

Expiration Date:

Document Type:

Date/Time Notarized: **AM** **PM**

Document Date:

Fee Charged:

Printed Name and Address of Witness:

1.

2.

Witness' Signature:

1.

2

Comments :

Record Number:

NOTARY RECORD

Printed Name and Address of Signer:	Phone Number:	Thumb Print:
	Email:	
	Signer's Signature:	

Service Performed:	Identification:		I.D. Number:	
☐ Oath	☐ I.D Card	☐ Credible Witness	Issued By:	
☐ Acknowledgment	☐ Drivers License	☐ Known Personally		
☐ Jurat	☐ Passport		Issued Date:	Expiration Date:
☐ Other:	☐ Other:			
Document Type:	Date/Time Notarized: AM PM		Document Date:	Fee Charged:

Printed Name and Address of Witness:	Witness' Signature:
1.	1.
2.	2.

Comments :	Record Number:

NOTARY RECORD

Printed Name and Address of Signer:	Phone Number:	Thumb Print:
	Email:	
	Signer's Signature:	

Service Performed:	Identification:		I.D. Number:	
☐ Oath	☐ I.D Card	☐ Credible Witness	Issued By:	
☐ Acknowledgment	☐ Drivers License	☐ Known Personally		
☐ Jurat	☐ Passport		Issued Date:	Expiration Date:
☐ Other:	☐ Other:			
Document Type:	Date/Time Notarized: AM PM		Document Date:	Fee Charged:

Printed Name and Address of Witness:	Witness' Signature:
1.	1.
2.	2

Comments :	Record Number:

NOTARY RECORD

Printed Name and Address of Signer:	Phone Number:	Thumb Print:
	Email:	
	Signer's Signature:	

Service Performed:	Identification:		I.D. Number:	
☐ Oath	☐ I.D Card	☐ Credible Witness		
☐ Acknowledgment	☐ Drivers License	☐ Known Personally	Issued By:	
☐ Jurat	☐ Passport			
☐ Other:	☐ Other:		Issued Date:	Expiration Date:
Document Type:	Date/Time Notarized: AM PM		Document Date:	Fee Charged:

Printed Name and Address of Witness:	Witness' Signature:
1.	1.
2.	2.

Comments :	Record Number:

NOTARY RECORD

Printed Name and Address of Signer:	Phone Number:	Thumb Print:
	Email:	
	Signer's Signature:	

Service Performed:	Identification:		I.D. Number:	
☐ Oath	☐ I.D Card	☐ Credible Witness		
☐ Acknowledgment	☐ Drivers License	☐ Known Personally	Issued By:	
☐ Jurat	☐ Passport			
☐ Other:	☐ Other:		Issued Date:	Expiration Date:
Document Type:	Date/Time Notarized: AM PM		Document Date:	Fee Charged:

Printed Name and Address of Witness:	Witness' Signature:
1.	1.
2.	2

Comments :	Record Number:

NOTARY RECORD

Printed Name and Address of Signer:

Phone Number:

Email:

Signer's Signature:

Thumb Print:

Service Performed:

- ☐ Oath
- ☐ Acknowledgment
- ☐ Jurat
- ☐ Other:

Identification:

- ☐ I.D Card
- ☐ Credible Witness
- ☐ Drivers License
- ☐ Known Personally
- ☐ Passport
- ☐ Other:

I.D. Number:

Issued By:

Issued Date:

Expiration Date:

Document Type:

Date/Time Notarized: **AM** **PM**

Document Date:

Fee Charged:

Printed Name and Address of Witness:

1.

2.

Witness' Signature:

1.

2.

Comments :

Record Number:

NOTARY RECORD

Printed Name and Address of Signer:

Phone Number:

Email:

Signer's Signature:

Thumb Print:

Service Performed:

- ☐ Oath
- ☐ Acknowledgment
- ☐ Jurat
- ☐ Other:

Identification:

- ☐ I.D Card
- ☐ Credible Witness
- ☐ Drivers License
- ☐ Known Personally
- ☐ Passport
- ☐ Other:

I.D. Number:

Issued By:

Issued Date:

Expiration Date:

Document Type:

Date/Time Notarized: **AM** **PM**

Document Date:

Fee Charged:

Printed Name and Address of Witness:

1.

2.

Witness' Signature:

1.

2

Comments :

Record Number:

NOTARY RECORD

Printed Name and Address of Signer:

Phone Number:

Email:

Signer's Signature:

Thumb Print:

Service Performed:

- ☐ Oath
- ☐ Acknowledgment
- ☐ Jurat
- ☐ Other:

Identification:

- ☐ I.D Card
- ☐ Credible Witness
- ☐ Drivers License
- ☐ Known Personally
- ☐ Passport
- ☐ Other:

I.D. Number:

Issued By:

Issued Date:

Expiration Date:

Document Type:

Date/Time Notarized: AM PM

Document Date:

Fee Charged:

Printed Name and Address of Witness:

1.

2.

Witness' Signature:

1.

2.

Comments :

Record Number:

NOTARY RECORD

Printed Name and Address of Signer:

Phone Number:

Email:

Signer's Signature:

Thumb Print:

Service Performed:

- ☐ Oath
- ☐ Acknowledgment
- ☐ Jurat
- ☐ Other:

Identification:

- ☐ I.D Card
- ☐ Credible Witness
- ☐ Drivers License
- ☐ Known Personally
- ☐ Passport
- ☐ Other:

I.D. Number:

Issued By:

Issued Date:

Expiration Date:

Document Type:

Date/Time Notarized: AM PM

Document Date:

Fee Charged:

Printed Name and Address of Witness:

1.

2.

Witness' Signature:

1.

2

Comments :

Record Number:

NOTARY RECORD

Printed Name and Address of Signer:	**Phone Number:**	**Thumb Print:**
	Email:	
	Signer's Signature:	

Service Performed: ☐ Oath ☐ Acknowledgment ☐ Jurat ☐ Other:	**Identification:** ☐ I.D Card ☐ Credible Witness ☐ Drivers License ☐ Known Personally ☐ Passport ☐ Other:	**I.D. Number:** **Issued By:** **Issued Date:** **Expiration Date:**
Document Type:	**Date/Time Notarized:** AM PM	**Document Date:** **Fee Charged:**

Printed Name and Address of Witness: **1.** **2.**	**Witness' Signature:** **1.** **2.**
Comments :	**Record Number:**

NOTARY RECORD

Printed Name and Address of Signer:	**Phone Number:**	**Thumb Print:**
	Email:	
	Signer's Signature:	

Service Performed: ☐ Oath ☐ Acknowledgment ☐ Jurat ☐ Other:	**Identification:** ☐ I.D Card ☐ Credible Witness ☐ Drivers License ☐ Known Personally ☐ Passport ☐ Other:	**I.D. Number:** **Issued By:** **Issued Date:** **Expiration Date:**
Document Type:	**Date/Time Notarized:** AM PM	**Document Date:** **Fee Charged:**

Printed Name and Address of Witness: **1.** **2.**	**Witness' Signature:** **1.** **2**
Comments :	**Record Number:**

NOTARY RECORD

Printed Name and Address of Signer:	**Phone Number:**	**Thumb Print:**
	Email:	
	Signer's Signature:	

Service Performed: ☐ Oath ☐ Acknowledgment ☐ Jurat ☐ Other:	**Identification:** ☐ I.D Card ☐ Credible Witness ☐ Drivers License ☐ Known Personally ☐ Passport ☐ Other:	**I.D. Number:**	
		Issued By:	
		Issued Date:	**Expiration Date:**
Document Type:	**Date/Time Notarized:** AM PM	**Document Date:**	**Fee Charged:**

Printed Name and Address of Witness: **1.** **2.**	**Witness' Signature:** **1.** **2.**

Comments :	**Record Number:**

NOTARY RECORD

Printed Name and Address of Signer:	**Phone Number:**	**Thumb Print:**
	Email:	
	Signer's Signature:	

Service Performed: ☐ Oath ☐ Acknowledgment ☐ Jurat ☐ Other:	**Identification:** ☐ I.D Card ☐ Credible Witness ☐ Drivers License ☐ Known Personally ☐ Passport ☐ Other:	**I.D. Number:**	
		Issued By:	
		Issued Date:	**Expiration Date:**
Document Type:	**Date/Time Notarized:** AM PM	**Document Date:**	**Fee Charged:**

Printed Name and Address of Witness: **1.** **2.**	**Witness' Signature:** **1.** **2**

Comments :	**Record Number:**

NOTARY RECORD

Printed Name and Address of Signer:	Phone Number:	Thumb Print:
	Email:	
	Signer's Signature:	

Service Performed:	Identification:		I.D. Number:	
☐ Oath	☐ I.D Card	☐ Credible Witness	Issued By:	
☐ Acknowledgment	☐ Drivers License	☐ Known Personally	Issued Date:	Expiration Date:
☐ Jurat	☐ Passport			
☐ Other:	☐ Other:			
Document Type:	Date/Time Notarized: AM PM		Document Date:	Fee Charged:

Printed Name and Address of Witness:	Witness' Signature:
1.	1.
2.	2.

Comments :	Record Number:

NOTARY RECORD

Printed Name and Address of Signer:	Phone Number:	Thumb Print:
	Email:	
	Signer's Signature:	

Service Performed:	Identification:		I.D. Number:	
☐ Oath	☐ I.D Card	☐ Credible Witness	Issued By:	
☐ Acknowledgment	☐ Drivers License	☐ Known Personally	Issued Date:	Expiration Date:
☐ Jurat	☐ Passport			
☐ Other:	☐ Other:			
Document Type:	Date/Time Notarized: AM PM		Document Date:	Fee Charged:

Printed Name and Address of Witness:	Witness' Signature:
1.	1.
2.	2

Comments :	Record Number:

NOTARY RECORD

Printed Name and Address of Signer:	**Phone Number:**	**Thumb Print:**
	Email:	
	Signer's Signature:	

Service Performed: ☐ Oath ☐ Acknowledgment ☐ Jurat ☐ Other:	**Identification:** ☐ I.D Card ☐ Credible Witness ☐ Drivers License ☐ Known Personally ☐ Passport ☐ Other:	**I.D. Number:**	
		Issued By:	
		Issued Date:	**Expiration Date:**
Document Type:	**Date/Time Notarized:** AM PM	**Document Date:**	**Fee Charged:**

Printed Name and Address of Witness: **1.** **2.**	**Witness' Signature:** **1.** **2.**
Comments :	**Record Number:**

NOTARY RECORD

Printed Name and Address of Signer:	**Phone Number:**	**Thumb Print:**
	Email:	
	Signer's Signature:	

Service Performed: ☐ Oath ☐ Acknowledgment ☐ Jurat ☐ Other:	**Identification:** ☐ I.D Card ☐ Credible Witness ☐ Drivers License ☐ Known Personally ☐ Passport ☐ Other:	**I.D. Number:**	
		Issued By:	
		Issued Date:	**Expiration Date:**
Document Type:	**Date/Time Notarized:** AM PM	**Document Date:**	**Fee Charged:**

Printed Name and Address of Witness: **1.** **2.**	**Witness' Signature:** **1.** **2**
Comments :	**Record Number:**

NOTARY RECORD

Printed Name and Address of Signer:	**Phone Number:**	**Thumb Print:**
	Email:	
	Signer's Signature:	

Service Performed: ☐ Oath ☐ Acknowledgment ☐ Jurat ☐ Other:	**Identification:** ☐ I.D Card ☐ Credible Witness ☐ Drivers License ☐ Known Personally ☐ Passport ☐ Other:	**I.D. Number:**	
		Issued By:	
		Issued Date:	**Expiration Date:**
Document Type:	**Date/Time Notarized:** **AM** **PM**	**Document Date:**	**Fee Charged:**

Printed Name and Address of Witness: **1.** **2.**	**Witness' Signature:** **1.** **2.**
Comments :	**Record Number:**

NOTARY RECORD

Printed Name and Address of Signer:	**Phone Number:**	**Thumb Print:**
	Email:	
	Signer's Signature:	

Service Performed: ☐ Oath ☐ Acknowledgment ☐ Jurat ☐ Other:	**Identification:** ☐ I.D Card ☐ Credible Witness ☐ Drivers License ☐ Known Personally ☐ Passport ☐ Other:	**I.D. Number:**	
		Issued By:	
		Issued Date:	**Expiration Date:**
Document Type:	**Date/Time Notarized:** **AM** **PM**	**Document Date:**	**Fee Charged:**

Printed Name and Address of Witness: **1.** **2.**	**Witness' Signature:** **1.** **2**
Comments :	**Record Number:**

NOTARY RECORD

Printed Name and Address of Signer:	Phone Number:	Thumb Print:
	Email:	
	Signer's Signature:	

Service Performed:	Identification:		I.D. Number:	
☐ Oath	☐ I.D Card	☐ Credible Witness	Issued By:	
☐ Acknowledgment	☐ Drivers License	☐ Known Personally		
☐ Jurat	☐ Passport		Issued Date:	Expiration Date:
☐ Other:	☐ Other:			
Document Type:	Date/Time Notarized:	AM PM	Document Date:	Fee Charged:

Printed Name and Address of Witness:	Witness' Signature:
1.	1.
2.	2.

Comments :	Record Number:

NOTARY RECORD

Printed Name and Address of Signer:	Phone Number:	Thumb Print:
	Email:	
	Signer's Signature:	

Service Performed:	Identification:		I.D. Number:	
☐ Oath	☐ I.D Card	☐ Credible Witness	Issued By:	
☐ Acknowledgment	☐ Drivers License	☐ Known Personally		
☐ Jurat	☐ Passport		Issued Date:	Expiration Date:
☐ Other:	☐ Other:			
Document Type:	Date/Time Notarized:	AM PM	Document Date:	Fee Charged:

Printed Name and Address of Witness:	Witness' Signature:
1.	1.
2.	2

Comments :	Record Number:

NOTARY RECORD

Printed Name and Address of Signer:	Phone Number:	Thumb Print:
	Email:	
	Signer's Signature:	

Service Performed:	Identification:		I.D. Number:	
☐ Oath	☐ I.D Card	☐ Credible Witness		
☐ Acknowledgment	☐ Drivers License	☐ Known Personally	Issued By:	
☐ Jurat	☐ Passport			
☐ Other:	☐ Other:		Issued Date:	Expiration Date:
Document Type:	Date/Time Notarized: AM PM		Document Date:	Fee Charged:

Printed Name and Address of Witness:	Witness' Signature:
1.	1.
2.	2.

Comments :	Record Number:

NOTARY RECORD

Printed Name and Address of Signer:	Phone Number:	Thumb Print:
	Email:	
	Signer's Signature:	

Service Performed:	Identification:		I.D. Number:	
☐ Oath	☐ I.D Card	☐ Credible Witness		
☐ Acknowledgment	☐ Drivers License	☐ Known Personally	Issued By:	
☐ Jurat	☐ Passport			
☐ Other:	☐ Other:		Issued Date:	Expiration Date:
Document Type:	Date/Time Notarized: AM PM		Document Date:	Fee Charged:

Printed Name and Address of Witness:	Witness' Signature:
1.	1.
2.	2

Comments :	Record Number:

NOTARY RECORD

Printed Name and Address of Signer:	Phone Number:	Thumb Print:
	Email:	
	Signer's Signature:	

Service Performed:	Identification:		I.D. Number:	
☐ Oath	☐ I.D Card	☐ Credible Witness	Issued By:	
☐ Acknowledgment	☐ Drivers License	☐ Known Personally	Issued Date:	Expiration Date:
☐ Jurat	☐ Passport			
☐ Other:	☐ Other:			
Document Type:	Date/Time Notarized: AM PM		Document Date:	Fee Charged:

Printed Name and Address of Witness:	Witness' Signature:
1.	1.
2.	2.

Comments :	Record Number:

NOTARY RECORD

Printed Name and Address of Signer:	Phone Number:	Thumb Print:
	Email:	
	Signer's Signature:	

Service Performed:	Identification:		I.D. Number:	
☐ Oath	☐ I.D Card	☐ Credible Witness	Issued By:	
☐ Acknowledgment	☐ Drivers License	☐ Known Personally	Issued Date:	Expiration Date:
☐ Jurat	☐ Passport			
☐ Other:	☐ Other:			
Document Type:	Date/Time Notarized: AM PM		Document Date:	Fee Charged:

Printed Name and Address of Witness:	Witness' Signature:
1.	1.
2.	2

Comments :	Record Number:

NOTARY RECORD

Printed Name and Address of Signer:	**Phone Number:**	**Thumb Print:**
	Email:	
	Signer's Signature:	

Service Performed: ☐ Oath ☐ Acknowledgment ☐ Jurat ☐ Other:	**Identification:** ☐ I.D Card ☐ Credible Witness ☐ Drivers License ☐ Known Personally ☐ Passport ☐ Other:	**I.D. Number:**	
		Issued By:	
		Issued Date:	**Expiration Date:**
Document Type:	**Date/Time Notarized:** AM PM	**Document Date:**	**Fee Charged:**

Printed Name and Address of Witness: **1.** **2.**	**Witness' Signature:** **1.** **2.**
Comments :	**Record Number:**

NOTARY RECORD

Printed Name and Address of Signer:	**Phone Number:**	**Thumb Print:**
	Email:	
	Signer's Signature:	

Service Performed: ☐ Oath ☐ Acknowledgment ☐ Jurat ☐ Other:	**Identification:** ☐ I.D Card ☐ Credible Witness ☐ Drivers License ☐ Known Personally ☐ Passport ☐ Other:	**I.D. Number:**	
		Issued By:	
		Issued Date:	**Expiration Date:**
Document Type:	**Date/Time Notarized:** AM PM	**Document Date:**	**Fee Charged:**

Printed Name and Address of Witness: **1.** **2.**	**Witness' Signature:** **1.** **2**
Comments :	**Record Number:**

NOTARY RECORD

Printed Name and Address of Signer:	Phone Number:	Thumb Print:
	Email:	
	Signer's Signature:	

Service Performed:	Identification:		I.D. Number:	
☐ Oath	☐ I.D Card	☐ Credible Witness		
☐ Acknowledgment	☐ Drivers License	☐ Known Personally	Issued By:	
☐ Jurat	☐ Passport			
☐ Other:	☐ Other:		Issued Date:	Expiration Date:
Document Type:	Date/Time Notarized: AM PM		Document Date:	Fee Charged:

Printed Name and Address of Witness:	Witness' Signature:
1.	1.
2.	2.

Comments :	Record Number:

NOTARY RECORD

Printed Name and Address of Signer:	Phone Number:	Thumb Print:
	Email:	
	Signer's Signature:	

Service Performed:	Identification:		I.D. Number:	
☐ Oath	☐ I.D Card	☐ Credible Witness		
☐ Acknowledgment	☐ Drivers License	☐ Known Personally	Issued By:	
☐ Jurat	☐ Passport			
☐ Other:	☐ Other:		Issued Date:	Expiration Date:
Document Type:	Date/Time Notarized: AM PM		Document Date:	Fee Charged:

Printed Name and Address of Witness:	Witness' Signature:
1.	1.
2.	2

Comments :	Record Number:

NOTARY RECORD

Printed Name and Address of Signer:	**Phone Number:**	**Thumb Print:**
	Email:	
	Signer's Signature:	

Service Performed: ☐ Oath ☐ Acknowledgment ☐ Jurat ☐ Other:	**Identification:** ☐ I.D Card ☐ Credible Witness ☐ Drivers License ☐ Known Personally ☐ Passport ☐ Other:	**I.D. Number:**	
		Issued By:	
		Issued Date:	**Expiration Date:**
Document Type:	**Date/Time Notarized:** AM PM	**Document Date:**	**Fee Charged:**

Printed Name and Address of Witness: **1.** **2.**	**Witness' Signature:** **1.** **2.**
Comments :	**Record Number:**

NOTARY RECORD

Printed Name and Address of Signer:	**Phone Number:**	**Thumb Print:**
	Email:	
	Signer's Signature:	

Service Performed: ☐ Oath ☐ Acknowledgment ☐ Jurat ☐ Other:	**Identification:** ☐ I.D Card ☐ Credible Witness ☐ Drivers License ☐ Known Personally ☐ Passport ☐ Other:	**I.D. Number:**	
		Issued By:	
		Issued Date:	**Expiration Date:**
Document Type:	**Date/Time Notarized:** AM PM	**Document Date:**	**Fee Charged:**

Printed Name and Address of Witness: **1.** **2.**	**Witness' Signature:** **1.** **2**
Comments :	**Record Number:**

NOTARY RECORD

Printed Name and Address of Signer:

Phone Number:

Email:

Signer's Signature:

Thumb Print:

Service Performed:

- ☐ Oath
- ☐ Acknowledgment
- ☐ Jurat
- ☐ Other:

Identification:

- ☐ I.D Card
- ☐ Credible Witness
- ☐ Drivers License
- ☐ Known Personally
- ☐ Passport
- ☐ Other:

I.D. Number:

Issued By:

Issued Date:

Expiration Date:

Document Type:

Date/Time Notarized: AM PM

Document Date:

Fee Charged:

Printed Name and Address of Witness:

1.

2.

Witness' Signature:

1.

2.

Comments :

Record Number:

NOTARY RECORD

Printed Name and Address of Signer:

Phone Number:

Email:

Signer's Signature:

Thumb Print:

Service Performed:

- ☐ Oath
- ☐ Acknowledgment
- ☐ Jurat
- ☐ Other:

Identification:

- ☐ I.D Card
- ☐ Credible Witness
- ☐ Drivers License
- ☐ Known Personally
- ☐ Passport
- ☐ Other:

I.D. Number:

Issued By:

Issued Date:

Expiration Date:

Document Type:

Date/Time Notarized: AM PM

Document Date:

Fee Charged:

Printed Name and Address of Witness:

1.

2.

Witness' Signature:

1.

2

Comments :

Record Number:

NOTARY RECORD

Printed Name and Address of Signer:	**Phone Number:** **Email:** **Signer's Signature:**	**Thumb Print:**

Service Performed: ☐ Oath ☐ Acknowledgment ☐ Jurat ☐ Other:	**Identification:** ☐ I.D Card ☐ Credible Witness ☐ Drivers License ☐ Known Personally ☐ Passport ☐ Other:	**I.D. Number:** **Issued By:** **Issued Date:**	**Expiration Date:**
Document Type:	**Date/Time Notarized:** AM PM	**Document Date:**	**Fee Charged:**

Printed Name and Address of Witness: **1.** **2.**	**Witness' Signature:** **1.** **2.**
Comments :	**Record Number:**

NOTARY RECORD

Printed Name and Address of Signer:	**Phone Number:** **Email:** **Signer's Signature:**	**Thumb Print:**

Service Performed: ☐ Oath ☐ Acknowledgment ☐ Jurat ☐ Other:	**Identification:** ☐ I.D Card ☐ Credible Witness ☐ Drivers License ☐ Known Personally ☐ Passport ☐ Other:	**I.D. Number:** **Issued By:** **Issued Date:**	**Expiration Date:**
Document Type:	**Date/Time Notarized:** AM PM	**Document Date:**	**Fee Charged:**

Printed Name and Address of Witness: **1.** **2.**	**Witness' Signature:** **1.** **2**
Comments :	**Record Number:**

NOTARY RECORD

Printed Name and Address of Signer:	Phone Number:	Thumb Print:
	Email:	
	Signer's Signature:	

Service Performed:	Identification:		I.D. Number:	
☐ Oath	☐ I.D Card	☐ Credible Witness	Issued By:	
☐ Acknowledgment	☐ Drivers License	☐ Known Personally	Issued Date:	Expiration Date:
☐ Jurat	☐ Passport			
☐ Other:	☐ Other:			
Document Type:	Date/Time Notarized: AM PM		Document Date:	Fee Charged:

Printed Name and Address of Witness:	Witness' Signature:
1.	1.
2.	2.

Comments :	Record Number:

NOTARY RECORD

Printed Name and Address of Signer:	Phone Number:	Thumb Print:
	Email:	
	Signer's Signature:	

Service Performed:	Identification:		I.D. Number:	
☐ Oath	☐ I.D Card	☐ Credible Witness	Issued By:	
☐ Acknowledgment	☐ Drivers License	☐ Known Personally	Issued Date:	Expiration Date:
☐ Jurat	☐ Passport			
☐ Other:	☐ Other:			
Document Type:	Date/Time Notarized: AM PM		Document Date:	Fee Charged:

Printed Name and Address of Witness:	Witness' Signature:
1.	1.
2.	2

Comments :	Record Number:

NOTARY RECORD

Printed Name and Address of Signer:	Phone Number:	Thumb Print:
	Email:	
	Signer's Signature:	

Service Performed:	Identification:		I.D. Number:	
☐ Oath	☐ I.D Card	☐ Credible Witness	Issued By:	
☐ Acknowledgment	☐ Drivers License	☐ Known Personally	Issued Date:	Expiration Date:
☐ Jurat	☐ Passport			
☐ Other:	☐ Other:			
Document Type:	Date/Time Notarized:	AM PM	Document Date:	Fee Charged:

Printed Name and Address of Witness:	Witness' Signature:
1.	1.
2.	2.

Comments :	Record Number:

NOTARY RECORD

Printed Name and Address of Signer:	Phone Number:	Thumb Print:
	Email:	
	Signer's Signature:	

Service Performed:	Identification:		I.D. Number:	
☐ Oath	☐ I.D Card	☐ Credible Witness	Issued By:	
☐ Acknowledgment	☐ Drivers License	☐ Known Personally	Issued Date:	Expiration Date:
☐ Jurat	☐ Passport			
☐ Other:	☐ Other:			
Document Type:	Date/Time Notarized:	AM PM	Document Date:	Fee Charged:

Printed Name and Address of Witness:	Witness' Signature:
1.	1.
2.	2

Comments :	Record Number:

NOTARY RECORD

Printed Name and Address of Signer:	**Phone Number:**	**Thumb Print:**
	Email:	
	Signer's Signature:	

Service Performed:	**Identification:**	**I.D. Number:**
☐ Oath	☐ I.D Card ☐ Credible Witness	**Issued By:**
☐ Acknowledgment	☐ Drivers License ☐ Known Personally	**Issued Date:** / **Expiration Date:**
☐ Jurat	☐ Passport	
☐ Other:	☐ Other:	
Document Type:	**Date/Time Notarized:** AM PM	**Document Date:** / **Fee Charged:**

Printed Name and Address of Witness:	**Witness' Signature:**
1.	**1.**
2.	**2.**

Comments :	**Record Number:**

NOTARY RECORD

Printed Name and Address of Signer:	**Phone Number:**	**Thumb Print:**
	Email:	
	Signer's Signature:	

Service Performed:	**Identification:**	**I.D. Number:**
☐ Oath	☐ I.D Card ☐ Credible Witness	**Issued By:**
☐ Acknowledgment	☐ Drivers License ☐ Known Personally	**Issued Date:** / **Expiration Date:**
☐ Jurat	☐ Passport	
☐ Other:	☐ Other:	
Document Type:	**Date/Time Notarized:** AM PM	**Document Date:** / **Fee Charged:**

Printed Name and Address of Witness:	**Witness' Signature:**
1.	**1.**
2.	**2**

Comments :	**Record Number:**

NOTARY RECORD

Printed Name and Address of Signer:	Phone Number:	Thumb Print:
	Email:	
	Signer's Signature:	

Service Performed:	Identification:		I.D. Number:	
☐ Oath	☐ I.D Card	☐ Credible Witness	Issued By:	
☐ Acknowledgment	☐ Drivers License	☐ Known Personally		
☐ Jurat	☐ Passport		Issued Date:	Expiration Date:
☐ Other:	☐ Other:			
Document Type:	Date/Time Notarized: AM PM		Document Date:	Fee Charged:

Printed Name and Address of Witness:	Witness' Signature:
1.	1.
2.	2.

Comments :	Record Number:

NOTARY RECORD

Printed Name and Address of Signer:	Phone Number:	Thumb Print:
	Email:	
	Signer's Signature:	

Service Performed:	Identification:		I.D. Number:	
☐ Oath	☐ I.D Card	☐ Credible Witness	Issued By:	
☐ Acknowledgment	☐ Drivers License	☐ Known Personally		
☐ Jurat	☐ Passport		Issued Date:	Expiration Date:
☐ Other:	☐ Other:			
Document Type:	Date/Time Notarized: AM PM		Document Date:	Fee Charged:

Printed Name and Address of Witness:	Witness' Signature:
1.	1.
2.	2

Comments :	Record Number:

NOTARY RECORD

Printed Name and Address of Signer:	**Phone Number:**	**Thumb Print:**
	Email:	
	Signer's Signature:	

Service Performed: ☐ Oath ☐ Acknowledgment ☐ Jurat ☐ Other:	**Identification:** ☐ I.D Card ☐ Credible Witness ☐ Drivers License ☐ Known Personally ☐ Passport ☐ Other:	**I.D. Number:**	
		Issued By:	
		Issued Date:	**Expiration Date:**
Document Type:	**Date/Time Notarized:** AM PM	**Document Date:**	**Fee Charged:**

Printed Name and Address of Witness: **1.** **2.**	**Witness' Signature:** **1.** **2.**

Comments :	**Record Number:**

NOTARY RECORD

Printed Name and Address of Signer:	**Phone Number:**	**Thumb Print:**
	Email:	
	Signer's Signature:	

Service Performed: ☐ Oath ☐ Acknowledgment ☐ Jurat ☐ Other:	**Identification:** ☐ I.D Card ☐ Credible Witness ☐ Drivers License ☐ Known Personally ☐ Passport ☐ Other:	**I.D. Number:**	
		Issued By:	
		Issued Date:	**Expiration Date:**
Document Type:	**Date/Time Notarized:** AM PM	**Document Date:**	**Fee Charged:**

Printed Name and Address of Witness: **1.** **2.**	**Witness' Signature:** **1.** **2**

Comments :	**Record Number:**

NOTARY RECORD

Printed Name and Address of Signer:	Phone Number:	Thumb Print:
	Email:	
	Signer's Signature:	

Service Performed:	Identification:		I.D. Number:	
☐ Oath	☐ I.D Card	☐ Credible Witness	Issued By:	
☐ Acknowledgment	☐ Drivers License	☐ Known Personally		
☐ Jurat	☐ Passport		Issued Date:	Expiration Date:
☐ Other:	☐ Other:			
Document Type:	Date/Time Notarized: AM PM		Document Date:	Fee Charged:

Printed Name and Address of Witness:	Witness' Signature:
1.	1.
2.	2.

Comments :	Record Number:

NOTARY RECORD

Printed Name and Address of Signer:	Phone Number:	Thumb Print:
	Email:	
	Signer's Signature:	

Service Performed:	Identification:		I.D. Number:	
☐ Oath	☐ I.D Card	☐ Credible Witness	Issued By:	
☐ Acknowledgment	☐ Drivers License	☐ Known Personally		
☐ Jurat	☐ Passport		Issued Date:	Expiration Date:
☐ Other:	☐ Other:			
Document Type:	Date/Time Notarized: AM PM		Document Date:	Fee Charged:

Printed Name and Address of Witness:	Witness' Signature:
1.	1.
2.	2

Comments :	Record Number:

NOTARY RECORD

Printed Name and Address of Signer:

Phone Number:

Email:

Signer's Signature:

Thumb Print:

Service Performed:

- ☐ Oath
- ☐ Acknowledgment
- ☐ Jurat
- ☐ Other:

Identification:

- ☐ I.D Card
- ☐ Credible Witness
- ☐ Drivers License
- ☐ Known Personally
- ☐ Passport
- ☐ Other:

I.D. Number:

Issued By:

Issued Date:

Expiration Date:

Document Type:

Date/Time Notarized: **AM** **PM**

Document Date:

Fee Charged:

Printed Name and Address of Witness:

1.

2.

Witness' Signature:

1.

2.

Comments :

Record Number:

NOTARY RECORD

Printed Name and Address of Signer:

Phone Number:

Email:

Signer's Signature:

Thumb Print:

Service Performed:

- ☐ Oath
- ☐ Acknowledgment
- ☐ Jurat
- ☐ Other:

Identification:

- ☐ I.D Card
- ☐ Credible Witness
- ☐ Drivers License
- ☐ Known Personally
- ☐ Passport
- ☐ Other:

I.D. Number:

Issued By:

Issued Date:

Expiration Date:

Document Type:

Date/Time Notarized: **AM** **PM**

Document Date:

Fee Charged:

Printed Name and Address of Witness:

1.

2.

Witness' Signature:

1.

2

Comments :

Record Number:

NOTARY RECORD

Printed Name and Address of Signer:	Phone Number:	Thumb Print:
	Email:	
	Signer's Signature:	

Service Performed:	Identification:		I.D. Number:	
☐ Oath	☐ I.D Card	☐ Credible Witness		
☐ Acknowledgment	☐ Drivers License	☐ Known Personally	Issued By:	
☐ Jurat	☐ Passport			
☐ Other:	☐ Other:		Issued Date:	Expiration Date:
Document Type:	Date/Time Notarized: AM PM		Document Date:	Fee Charged:

Printed Name and Address of Witness:	Witness' Signature:
1.	1.
2.	2.

Comments :	Record Number:

NOTARY RECORD

Printed Name and Address of Signer:	Phone Number:	Thumb Print:
	Email:	
	Signer's Signature:	

Service Performed:	Identification:		I.D. Number:	
☐ Oath	☐ I.D Card	☐ Credible Witness		
☐ Acknowledgment	☐ Drivers License	☐ Known Personally	Issued By:	
☐ Jurat	☐ Passport			
☐ Other:	☐ Other:		Issued Date:	Expiration Date:
Document Type:	Date/Time Notarized: AM PM		Document Date:	Fee Charged:

Printed Name and Address of Witness:	Witness' Signature:
1.	1.
2.	2

Comments :	Record Number:

NOTARY RECORD

Printed Name and Address of Signer:	Phone Number:	Thumb Print:
	Email:	
	Signer's Signature:	

Service Performed:	Identification:		I.D. Number:	
☐ Oath	☐ I.D Card	☐ Credible Witness		
☐ Acknowledgment	☐ Drivers License	☐ Known Personally	Issued By:	
☐ Jurat	☐ Passport			
☐ Other:	☐ Other:		Issued Date:	Expiration Date:
Document Type:	Date/Time Notarized: AM PM		Document Date:	Fee Charged:

Printed Name and Address of Witness:	Witness' Signature:
1.	1.
2.	2.

Comments :	Record Number:

NOTARY RECORD

Printed Name and Address of Signer:	Phone Number:	Thumb Print:
	Email:	
	Signer's Signature:	

Service Performed:	Identification:		I.D. Number:	
☐ Oath	☐ I.D Card	☐ Credible Witness		
☐ Acknowledgment	☐ Drivers License	☐ Known Personally	Issued By:	
☐ Jurat	☐ Passport			
☐ Other:	☐ Other:		Issued Date:	Expiration Date:
Document Type:	Date/Time Notarized: AM PM		Document Date:	Fee Charged:

Printed Name and Address of Witness:	Witness' Signature:
1.	1.
2.	2

Comments :	Record Number:

NOTARY RECORD

Printed Name and Address of Signer:	Phone Number:	Thumb Print:
	Email:	
	Signer's Signature:	

Service Performed:	Identification:		I.D. Number:	
☐ Oath	☐ I.D Card	☐ Credible Witness		
☐ Acknowledgment	☐ Drivers License	☐ Known Personally	Issued By:	
☐ Jurat	☐ Passport		Issued Date:	Expiration Date:
☐ Other:	☐ Other:			
Document Type:	Date/Time Notarized:	AM PM	Document Date:	Fee Charged:

Printed Name and Address of Witness:	Witness' Signature:
1.	1.
2.	2.

Comments :	Record Number:

NOTARY RECORD

Printed Name and Address of Signer:	Phone Number:	Thumb Print:
	Email:	
	Signer's Signature:	

Service Performed:	Identification:		I.D. Number:	
☐ Oath	☐ I.D Card	☐ Credible Witness		
☐ Acknowledgment	☐ Drivers License	☐ Known Personally	Issued By:	
☐ Jurat	☐ Passport		Issued Date:	Expiration Date:
☐ Other:	☐ Other:			
Document Type:	Date/Time Notarized:	AM PM	Document Date:	Fee Charged:

Printed Name and Address of Witness:	Witness' Signature:
1.	1.
2.	2

Comments :	Record Number:

NOTARY RECORD

Printed Name and Address of Signer:

Phone Number:

Email:

Signer's Signature:

Thumb Print:

Service Performed:

- ☐ Oath
- ☐ Acknowledgment
- ☐ Jurat
- ☐ Other:

Identification:

- ☐ I.D Card
- ☐ Credible Witness
- ☐ Drivers License
- ☐ Known Personally
- ☐ Passport
- ☐ Other:

I.D. Number:

Issued By:

Issued Date:

Expiration Date:

Document Type:

Date/Time Notarized: **AM** **PM**

Document Date:

Fee Charged:

Printed Name and Address of Witness:

1.

2.

Witness' Signature:

1.

2.

Comments :

Record Number:

NOTARY RECORD

Printed Name and Address of Signer:

Phone Number:

Email:

Signer's Signature:

Thumb Print:

Service Performed:

- ☐ Oath
- ☐ Acknowledgment
- ☐ Jurat
- ☐ Other:

Identification:

- ☐ I.D Card
- ☐ Credible Witness
- ☐ Drivers License
- ☐ Known Personally
- ☐ Passport
- ☐ Other:

I.D. Number:

Issued By:

Issued Date:

Expiration Date:

Document Type:

Date/Time Notarized: **AM** **PM**

Document Date:

Fee Charged:

Printed Name and Address of Witness:

1.

2.

Witness' Signature:

1.

2

Comments :

Record Number:

NOTARY RECORD

Printed Name and Address of Signer:	Phone Number:	Thumb Print:
	Email:	
	Signer's Signature:	

Service Performed:	Identification:		I.D. Number:	
☐ Oath	☐ I.D Card	☐ Credible Witness	Issued By:	
☐ Acknowledgment	☐ Drivers License	☐ Known Personally	Issued Date:	Expiration Date:
☐ Jurat	☐ Passport			
☐ Other:	☐ Other:			
Document Type:	Date/Time Notarized:	AM PM	Document Date:	Fee Charged:

Printed Name and Address of Witness:	Witness' Signature:
1.	1.
2.	2.

Comments :	Record Number:

NOTARY RECORD

Printed Name and Address of Signer:	Phone Number:	Thumb Print:
	Email:	
	Signer's Signature:	

Service Performed:	Identification:		I.D. Number:	
☐ Oath	☐ I.D Card	☐ Credible Witness	Issued By:	
☐ Acknowledgment	☐ Drivers License	☐ Known Personally	Issued Date:	Expiration Date:
☐ Jurat	☐ Passport			
☐ Other:	☐ Other:			
Document Type:	Date/Time Notarized:	AM PM	Document Date:	Fee Charged:

Printed Name and Address of Witness:	Witness' Signature:
1.	1.
2.	2

Comments :	Record Number:

NOTARY RECORD

Printed Name and Address of Signer:	**Phone Number:**	**Thumb Print:**
	Email:	
	Signer's Signature:	

Service Performed: ☐ Oath ☐ Acknowledgment ☐ Jurat ☐ Other:	**Identification:** ☐ I.D Card ☐ Credible Witness ☐ Drivers License ☐ Known Personally ☐ Passport ☐ Other:	**I.D. Number:**	
		Issued By:	
		Issued Date:	**Expiration Date:**
Document Type:	**Date/Time Notarized:** AM PM	**Document Date:**	**Fee Charged:**

Printed Name and Address of Witness: **1.** **2.**	**Witness' Signature:** **1.** **2.**
Comments :	**Record Number:**

NOTARY RECORD

Printed Name and Address of Signer:	**Phone Number:**	**Thumb Print:**
	Email:	
	Signer's Signature:	

Service Performed: ☐ Oath ☐ Acknowledgment ☐ Jurat ☐ Other:	**Identification:** ☐ I.D Card ☐ Credible Witness ☐ Drivers License ☐ Known Personally ☐ Passport ☐ Other:	**I.D. Number:**	
		Issued By:	
		Issued Date:	**Expiration Date:**
Document Type:	**Date/Time Notarized:** AM PM	**Document Date:**	**Fee Charged:**

Printed Name and Address of Witness: **1.** **2.**	**Witness' Signature:** **1.** **2**
Comments :	**Record Number:**

NOTARY RECORD

Printed Name and Address of Signer:	Phone Number:	Thumb Print:
	Email:	
	Signer's Signature:	

Service Performed:	Identification:		I.D. Number:	
☐ Oath	☐ I.D Card	☐ Credible Witness		
☐ Acknowledgment	☐ Drivers License	☐ Known Personally	Issued By:	
☐ Jurat	☐ Passport			
☐ Other:	☐ Other:		Issued Date:	Expiration Date:
Document Type:	Date/Time Notarized:	AM PM	Document Date:	Fee Charged:

Printed Name and Address of Witness:	Witness' Signature:
1.	1.
2.	2.

Comments :	Record Number:

NOTARY RECORD

Printed Name and Address of Signer:	Phone Number:	Thumb Print:
	Email:	
	Signer's Signature:	

Service Performed:	Identification:		I.D. Number:	
☐ Oath	☐ I.D Card	☐ Credible Witness		
☐ Acknowledgment	☐ Drivers License	☐ Known Personally	Issued By:	
☐ Jurat	☐ Passport			
☐ Other:	☐ Other:		Issued Date:	Expiration Date:
Document Type:	Date/Time Notarized:	AM PM	Document Date:	Fee Charged:

Printed Name and Address of Witness:	Witness' Signature:
1.	1.
2.	2

Comments :	Record Number:

NOTARY RECORD

Printed Name and Address of Signer:	Phone Number:	Thumb Print:
	Email:	
	Signer's Signature:	

Service Performed:	Identification:		I.D. Number:	
☐ Oath	☐ I.D Card	☐ Credible Witness	Issued By:	
☐ Acknowledgment	☐ Drivers License	☐ Known Personally		
☐ Jurat	☐ Passport		Issued Date:	Expiration Date:
☐ Other:	☐ Other:			
Document Type:	Date/Time Notarized: AM PM		Document Date:	Fee Charged:

Printed Name and Address of Witness:	Witness' Signature:
1.	1.
2.	2.

Comments :	Record Number:

NOTARY RECORD

Printed Name and Address of Signer:	Phone Number:	Thumb Print:
	Email:	
	Signer's Signature:	

Service Performed:	Identification:		I.D. Number:	
☐ Oath	☐ I.D Card	☐ Credible Witness	Issued By:	
☐ Acknowledgment	☐ Drivers License	☐ Known Personally		
☐ Jurat	☐ Passport		Issued Date:	Expiration Date:
☐ Other:	☐ Other:			
Document Type:	Date/Time Notarized: AM PM		Document Date:	Fee Charged:

Printed Name and Address of Witness:	Witness' Signature:
1.	1.
2.	2

Comments :	Record Number:

NOTARY RECORD

Printed Name and Address of Signer:	Phone Number:	Thumb Print:
	Email:	
	Signer's Signature:	

Service Performed:	Identification:		I.D. Number:	
☐ Oath	☐ I.D Card	☐ Credible Witness		
☐ Acknowledgment	☐ Drivers License	☐ Known Personally	Issued By:	
☐ Jurat	☐ Passport			
☐ Other:	☐ Other:		Issued Date:	Expiration Date:
Document Type:	Date/Time Notarized: AM PM		Document Date:	Fee Charged:

Printed Name and Address of Witness:	Witness' Signature:
1.	1.
2.	2.

Comments :	Record Number:

NOTARY RECORD

Printed Name and Address of Signer:	Phone Number:	Thumb Print:
	Email:	
	Signer's Signature:	

Service Performed:	Identification:		I.D. Number:	
☐ Oath	☐ I.D Card	☐ Credible Witness		
☐ Acknowledgment	☐ Drivers License	☐ Known Personally	Issued By:	
☐ Jurat	☐ Passport			
☐ Other:	☐ Other:		Issued Date:	Expiration Date:
Document Type:	Date/Time Notarized: AM PM		Document Date:	Fee Charged:

Printed Name and Address of Witness:	Witness' Signature:
1.	1.
2.	2

Comments :	Record Number:

NOTARY RECORD

Printed Name and Address of Signer:	Phone Number:	Thumb Print:
	Email:	
	Signer's Signature:	

Service Performed:	Identification:		I.D. Number:	
☐ Oath	☐ I.D Card	☐ Credible Witness	Issued By:	
☐ Acknowledgment	☐ Drivers License	☐ Known Personally		
☐ Jurat	☐ Passport		Issued Date:	Expiration Date:
☐ Other:	☐ Other:			
Document Type:	Date/Time Notarized: AM PM		Document Date:	Fee Charged:

Printed Name and Address of Witness:	Witness' Signature:
1.	1.
2.	2.

Comments :	Record Number:

NOTARY RECORD

Printed Name and Address of Signer:	Phone Number:	Thumb Print:
	Email:	
	Signer's Signature:	

Service Performed:	Identification:		I.D. Number:	
☐ Oath	☐ I.D Card	☐ Credible Witness	Issued By:	
☐ Acknowledgment	☐ Drivers License	☐ Known Personally		
☐ Jurat	☐ Passport		Issued Date:	Expiration Date:
☐ Other:	☐ Other:			
Document Type:	Date/Time Notarized: AM PM		Document Date:	Fee Charged:

Printed Name and Address of Witness:	Witness' Signature:
1.	1.
2.	2

Comments :	Record Number:

NOTARY RECORD

Printed Name and Address of Signer:	**Phone Number:**	**Thumb Print:**
	Email:	
	Signer's Signature:	

Service Performed: ☐ Oath ☐ Acknowledgment ☐ Jurat ☐ Other:	**Identification:** ☐ I.D Card ☐ Credible Witness ☐ Drivers License ☐ Known Personally ☐ Passport ☐ Other:	**I.D. Number:**	
		Issued By:	
		Issued Date:	**Expiration Date:**
Document Type:	**Date/Time Notarized:** AM PM	**Document Date:**	**Fee Charged:**

Printed Name and Address of Witness: **1.** **2.**	**Witness' Signature:** **1.** **2.**
Comments :	**Record Number:**

NOTARY RECORD

Printed Name and Address of Signer:	**Phone Number:**	**Thumb Print:**
	Email:	
	Signer's Signature:	

Service Performed: ☐ Oath ☐ Acknowledgment ☐ Jurat ☐ Other:	**Identification:** ☐ I.D Card ☐ Credible Witness ☐ Drivers License ☐ Known Personally ☐ Passport ☐ Other:	**I.D. Number:**	
		Issued By:	
		Issued Date:	**Expiration Date:**
Document Type:	**Date/Time Notarized:** AM PM	**Document Date:**	**Fee Charged:**

Printed Name and Address of Witness: **1.** **2.**	**Witness' Signature:** **1.** **2**
Comments :	**Record Number:**

NOTARY RECORD

Printed Name and Address of Signer:	Phone Number:	Thumb Print:
	Email:	
	Signer's Signature:	

Service Performed:	Identification:		I.D. Number:	
☐ Oath	☐ I.D Card	☐ Credible Witness	Issued By:	
☐ Acknowledgment	☐ Drivers License	☐ Known Personally	Issued Date:	Expiration Date:
☐ Jurat	☐ Passport			
☐ Other:	☐ Other:			
Document Type:	Date/Time Notarized:	AM PM	Document Date:	Fee Charged:

Printed Name and Address of Witness:	Witness' Signature:
1.	1.
2.	2.

Comments :	Record Number:

NOTARY RECORD

Printed Name and Address of Signer:	Phone Number:	Thumb Print:
	Email:	
	Signer's Signature:	

Service Performed:	Identification:		I.D. Number:	
☐ Oath	☐ I.D Card	☐ Credible Witness	Issued By:	
☐ Acknowledgment	☐ Drivers License	☐ Known Personally	Issued Date:	Expiration Date:
☐ Jurat	☐ Passport			
☐ Other:	☐ Other:			
Document Type:	Date/Time Notarized:	AM PM	Document Date:	Fee Charged:

Printed Name and Address of Witness:	Witness' Signature:
1.	1.
2.	2

Comments :	Record Number:

NOTARY RECORD

Printed Name and Address of Signer:	Phone Number:	Thumb Print:
	Email:	
	Signer's Signature:	

Service Performed:	Identification:		I.D. Number:	
☐ Oath	☐ I.D Card	☐ Credible Witness	Issued By:	
☐ Acknowledgment	☐ Drivers License	☐ Known Personally		
☐ Jurat	☐ Passport		Issued Date:	Expiration Date:
☐ Other:	☐ Other:			
Document Type:	Date/Time Notarized:	AM PM	Document Date:	Fee Charged:

Printed Name and Address of Witness:	Witness' Signature:
1.	1.
2.	2.

Comments :	Record Number:

NOTARY RECORD

Printed Name and Address of Signer:	Phone Number:	Thumb Print:
	Email:	
	Signer's Signature:	

Service Performed:	Identification:		I.D. Number:	
☐ Oath	☐ I.D Card	☐ Credible Witness	Issued By:	
☐ Acknowledgment	☐ Drivers License	☐ Known Personally		
☐ Jurat	☐ Passport		Issued Date:	Expiration Date:
☐ Other:	☐ Other:			
Document Type:	Date/Time Notarized:	AM PM	Document Date:	Fee Charged:

Printed Name and Address of Witness:	Witness' Signature:
1.	1.
2.	2

Comments :	Record Number:

NOTARY RECORD

Printed Name and Address of Signer:	Phone Number:	Thumb Print:
	Email:	
	Signer's Signature:	

Service Performed:	Identification:		I.D. Number:	
☐ Oath	☐ I.D Card	☐ Credible Witness		
☐ Acknowledgment	☐ Drivers License	☐ Known Personally	Issued By:	
☐ Jurat	☐ Passport		Issued Date:	Expiration Date:
☐ Other:	☐ Other:			
Document Type:	Date/Time Notarized:	AM PM	Document Date:	Fee Charged:

Printed Name and Address of Witness:	Witness' Signature:
1.	1.
2.	2.

Comments :	Record Number:

NOTARY RECORD

Printed Name and Address of Signer:	Phone Number:	Thumb Print:
	Email:	
	Signer's Signature:	

Service Performed:	Identification:		I.D. Number:	
☐ Oath	☐ I.D Card	☐ Credible Witness		
☐ Acknowledgment	☐ Drivers License	☐ Known Personally	Issued By:	
☐ Jurat	☐ Passport		Issued Date:	Expiration Date:
☐ Other:	☐ Other:			
Document Type:	Date/Time Notarized:	AM PM	Document Date:	Fee Charged:

Printed Name and Address of Witness:	Witness' Signature:
1.	1.
2.	2

Comments :	Record Number:

NOTARY RECORD

Printed Name and Address of Signer:	Phone Number:	Thumb Print:
	Email:	
	Signer's Signature:	

Service Performed:	Identification:		I.D. Number:	
☐ Oath	☐ I.D Card	☐ Credible Witness	Issued By:	
☐ Acknowledgment	☐ Drivers License	☐ Known Personally	Issued Date:	Expiration Date:
☐ Jurat	☐ Passport			
☐ Other:	☐ Other:			
Document Type:	Date/Time Notarized: AM PM		Document Date:	Fee Charged:

Printed Name and Address of Witness:	Witness' Signature:
1.	1.
2.	2.

Comments :	Record Number:

NOTARY RECORD

Printed Name and Address of Signer:	Phone Number:	Thumb Print:
	Email:	
	Signer's Signature:	

Service Performed:	Identification:		I.D. Number:	
☐ Oath	☐ I.D Card	☐ Credible Witness	Issued By:	
☐ Acknowledgment	☐ Drivers License	☐ Known Personally	Issued Date:	Expiration Date:
☐ Jurat	☐ Passport			
☐ Other:	☐ Other:			
Document Type:	Date/Time Notarized: AM PM		Document Date:	Fee Charged:

Printed Name and Address of Witness:	Witness' Signature:
1.	1.
2.	2

Comments :	Record Number:

NOTARY RECORD

Printed Name and Address of Signer:	Phone Number:	Thumb Print:
	Email:	
	Signer's Signature:	

Service Performed:	Identification:		I.D. Number:	
☐ Oath	☐ I.D Card	☐ Credible Witness	Issued By:	
☐ Acknowledgment	☐ Drivers License	☐ Known Personally	Issued Date:	Expiration Date:
☐ Jurat	☐ Passport			
☐ Other:	☐ Other:			
Document Type:	Date/Time Notarized: AM PM		Document Date:	Fee Charged:

Printed Name and Address of Witness:	Witness' Signature:
1.	1.
2.	2.

Comments :	Record Number:

NOTARY RECORD

Printed Name and Address of Signer:	Phone Number:	Thumb Print:
	Email:	
	Signer's Signature:	

Service Performed:	Identification:		I.D. Number:	
☐ Oath	☐ I.D Card	☐ Credible Witness	Issued By:	
☐ Acknowledgment	☐ Drivers License	☐ Known Personally	Issued Date:	Expiration Date:
☐ Jurat	☐ Passport			
☐ Other:	☐ Other:			
Document Type:	Date/Time Notarized: AM PM		Document Date:	Fee Charged:

Printed Name and Address of Witness:	Witness' Signature:
1.	1.
2.	2

Comments :	Record Number:

NOTARY RECORD

Printed Name and Address of Signer:	Phone Number:	Thumb Print:
	Email:	
	Signer's Signature:	

Service Performed:	Identification:		I.D. Number:	
☐ Oath	☐ I.D Card	☐ Credible Witness		
☐ Acknowledgment	☐ Drivers License	☐ Known Personally	Issued By:	
☐ Jurat	☐ Passport			
☐ Other:	☐ Other:		Issued Date:	Expiration Date:
Document Type:	Date/Time Notarized: AM PM		Document Date:	Fee Charged:

Printed Name and Address of Witness:	Witness' Signature:
1.	1.
2.	2.

Comments :	Record Number:

NOTARY RECORD

Printed Name and Address of Signer:	Phone Number:	Thumb Print:
	Email:	
	Signer's Signature:	

Service Performed:	Identification:		I.D. Number:	
☐ Oath	☐ I.D Card	☐ Credible Witness		
☐ Acknowledgment	☐ Drivers License	☐ Known Personally	Issued By:	
☐ Jurat	☐ Passport			
☐ Other:	☐ Other:		Issued Date:	Expiration Date:
Document Type:	Date/Time Notarized: AM PM		Document Date:	Fee Charged:

Printed Name and Address of Witness:	Witness' Signature:
1.	1.
2.	2

Comments :	Record Number:

NOTARY RECORD

Printed Name and Address of Signer:	**Phone Number:**	**Thumb Print:**
	Email:	
	Signer's Signature:	

Service Performed: ☐ Oath ☐ Acknowledgment ☐ Jurat ☐ Other:	**Identification:** ☐ I.D Card ☐ Credible Witness ☐ Drivers License ☐ Known Personally ☐ Passport ☐ Other:	**I.D. Number:**	
		Issued By:	
		Issued Date:	**Expiration Date:**
Document Type:	**Date/Time Notarized:** AM PM	**Document Date:**	**Fee Charged:**

Printed Name and Address of Witness:	**Witness' Signature:**
1.	**1.**
2.	**2.**

Comments :	**Record Number:**

NOTARY RECORD

Printed Name and Address of Signer:	**Phone Number:**	**Thumb Print:**
	Email:	
	Signer's Signature:	

Service Performed: ☐ Oath ☐ Acknowledgment ☐ Jurat ☐ Other:	**Identification:** ☐ I.D Card ☐ Credible Witness ☐ Drivers License ☐ Known Personally ☐ Passport ☐ Other:	**I.D. Number:**	
		Issued By:	
		Issued Date:	**Expiration Date:**
Document Type:	**Date/Time Notarized:** AM PM	**Document Date:**	**Fee Charged:**

Printed Name and Address of Witness:	**Witness' Signature:**
1.	**1.**
2.	**2**

Comments :	**Record Number:**

NOTARY RECORD

Printed Name and Address of Signer:	Phone Number:	Thumb Print:
	Email:	
	Signer's Signature:	

Service Performed:	Identification:		I.D. Number:	
☐ Oath	☐ I.D Card	☐ Credible Witness		
☐ Acknowledgment	☐ Drivers License	☐ Known Personally	Issued By:	
☐ Jurat	☐ Passport			
☐ Other:	☐ Other:		Issued Date:	Expiration Date:
Document Type:	Date/Time Notarized: AM PM		Document Date:	Fee Charged:

Printed Name and Address of Witness:	Witness' Signature:
1.	1.
2.	2.

Comments :	Record Number:

NOTARY RECORD

Printed Name and Address of Signer:	Phone Number:	Thumb Print:
	Email:	
	Signer's Signature:	

Service Performed:	Identification:		I.D. Number:	
☐ Oath	☐ I.D Card	☐ Credible Witness		
☐ Acknowledgment	☐ Drivers License	☐ Known Personally	Issued By:	
☐ Jurat	☐ Passport			
☐ Other:	☐ Other:		Issued Date:	Expiration Date:
Document Type:	Date/Time Notarized: AM PM		Document Date:	Fee Charged:

Printed Name and Address of Witness:	Witness' Signature:
1.	1.
2.	2

Comments :	Record Number:

NOTARY RECORD

Printed Name and Address of Signer:	Phone Number:	Thumb Print:
	Email:	
	Signer's Signature:	

Service Performed:	Identification:		I.D. Number:	
☐ Oath	☐ I.D Card	☐ Credible Witness	Issued By:	
☐ Acknowledgment	☐ Drivers License	☐ Known Personally	Issued Date:	Expiration Date:
☐ Jurat	☐ Passport			
☐ Other:	☐ Other:			
Document Type:	Date/Time Notarized: AM PM		Document Date:	Fee Charged:

Printed Name and Address of Witness:	Witness' Signature:
1.	1.
2.	2.

Comments :	Record Number:

NOTARY RECORD

Printed Name and Address of Signer:	Phone Number:	Thumb Print:
	Email:	
	Signer's Signature:	

Service Performed:	Identification:		I.D. Number:	
☐ Oath	☐ I.D Card	☐ Credible Witness	Issued By:	
☐ Acknowledgment	☐ Drivers License	☐ Known Personally	Issued Date:	Expiration Date:
☐ Jurat	☐ Passport			
☐ Other:	☐ Other:			
Document Type:	Date/Time Notarized: AM PM		Document Date:	Fee Charged:

Printed Name and Address of Witness:	Witness' Signature:
1.	1.
2.	2

Comments :	Record Number:

NOTARY RECORD

Printed Name and Address of Signer:	**Phone Number:**	**Thumb Print:**
	Email:	
	Signer's Signature:	

Service Performed: ☐ Oath ☐ Acknowledgment ☐ Jurat ☐ Other:	**Identification:** ☐ I.D Card ☐ Credible Witness ☐ Drivers License ☐ Known Personally ☐ Passport ☐ Other:	**I.D. Number:**	
		Issued By:	
		Issued Date:	**Expiration Date:**
Document Type:	**Date/Time Notarized:** AM PM	**Document Date:**	**Fee Charged:**

Printed Name and Address of Witness: **1.** **2.**	**Witness' Signature:** **1.** **2.**
Comments :	**Record Number:**

NOTARY RECORD

Printed Name and Address of Signer:	**Phone Number:**	**Thumb Print:**
	Email:	
	Signer's Signature:	

Service Performed: ☐ Oath ☐ Acknowledgment ☐ Jurat ☐ Other:	**Identification:** ☐ I.D Card ☐ Credible Witness ☐ Drivers License ☐ Known Personally ☐ Passport ☐ Other:	**I.D. Number:**	
		Issued By:	
		Issued Date:	**Expiration Date:**
Document Type:	**Date/Time Notarized:** AM PM	**Document Date:**	**Fee Charged:**

Printed Name and Address of Witness: **1.** **2.**	**Witness' Signature:** **1.** **2**
Comments :	**Record Number:**

NOTARY RECORD

Printed Name and Address of Signer:

Phone Number:

Email:

Signer's Signature:

Thumb Print:

Service Performed:

- ☐ Oath
- ☐ Acknowledgment
- ☐ Jurat
- ☐ Other:

Identification:

- ☐ I.D Card
- ☐ Credible Witness
- ☐ Drivers License
- ☐ Known Personally
- ☐ Passport
- ☐ Other:

I.D. Number:

Issued By:

Issued Date:

Expiration Date:

Document Type:

Date/Time Notarized: **AM** **PM**

Document Date:

Fee Charged:

Printed Name and Address of Witness:

1.

2.

Witness' Signature:

1.

2.

Comments :

Record Number:

NOTARY RECORD

Printed Name and Address of Signer:

Phone Number:

Email:

Signer's Signature:

Thumb Print:

Service Performed:

- ☐ Oath
- ☐ Acknowledgment
- ☐ Jurat
- ☐ Other:

Identification:

- ☐ I.D Card
- ☐ Credible Witness
- ☐ Drivers License
- ☐ Known Personally
- ☐ Passport
- ☐ Other:

I.D. Number:

Issued By:

Issued Date:

Expiration Date:

Document Type:

Date/Time Notarized: **AM** **PM**

Document Date:

Fee Charged:

Printed Name and Address of Witness:

1.

2.

Witness' Signature:

1.

2

Comments :

Record Number:

NOTARY RECORD

Printed Name and Address of Signer:	Phone Number:	Thumb Print:
	Email:	
	Signer's Signature:	

Service Performed:	Identification:		I.D. Number:	
☐ Oath	☐ I.D Card	☐ Credible Witness		
☐ Acknowledgment	☐ Drivers License	☐ Known Personally	Issued By:	
☐ Jurat	☐ Passport			
☐ Other:	☐ Other:		Issued Date:	Expiration Date:
Document Type:	Date/Time Notarized: AM PM		Document Date:	Fee Charged:

Printed Name and Address of Witness:	Witness' Signature:
1.	1.
2.	2.

Comments :	Record Number:

NOTARY RECORD

Printed Name and Address of Signer:	Phone Number:	Thumb Print:
	Email:	
	Signer's Signature:	

Service Performed:	Identification:		I.D. Number:	
☐ Oath	☐ I.D Card	☐ Credible Witness		
☐ Acknowledgment	☐ Drivers License	☐ Known Personally	Issued By:	
☐ Jurat	☐ Passport			
☐ Other:	☐ Other:		Issued Date:	Expiration Date:
Document Type:	Date/Time Notarized: AM PM		Document Date:	Fee Charged:

Printed Name and Address of Witness:	Witness' Signature:
1.	1.
2.	2

Comments :	Record Number:

NOTARY RECORD

Printed Name and Address of Signer:	**Phone Number:**	**Thumb Print:**
	Email:	
	Signer's Signature:	

Service Performed: ☐ Oath ☐ Acknowledgment ☐ Jurat ☐ Other:	**Identification:** ☐ I.D Card ☐ Credible Witness ☐ Drivers License ☐ Known Personally ☐ Passport ☐ Other:	**I.D. Number:** **Issued By:** **Issued Date:** **Expiration Date:**
Document Type:	**Date/Time Notarized:** AM PM	**Document Date:** **Fee Charged:**

Printed Name and Address of Witness: **1.** **2.**	**Witness' Signature:** **1.** **2.**
Comments :	**Record Number:**

NOTARY RECORD

Printed Name and Address of Signer:	**Phone Number:**	**Thumb Print:**
	Email:	
	Signer's Signature:	

Service Performed: ☐ Oath ☐ Acknowledgment ☐ Jurat ☐ Other:	**Identification:** ☐ I.D Card ☐ Credible Witness ☐ Drivers License ☐ Known Personally ☐ Passport ☐ Other:	**I.D. Number:** **Issued By:** **Issued Date:** **Expiration Date:**
Document Type:	**Date/Time Notarized:** AM PM	**Document Date:** **Fee Charged:**

Printed Name and Address of Witness: **1.** **2.**	**Witness' Signature:** **1.** **2**
Comments :	**Record Number:**

NOTARY RECORD

Printed Name and Address of Signer:

Phone Number:

Email:

Signer's Signature:

Thumb Print:

Service Performed:

- ☐ Oath
- ☐ Acknowledgment
- ☐ Jurat
- ☐ Other:

Identification:

- ☐ I.D Card
- ☐ Credible Witness
- ☐ Drivers License
- ☐ Known Personally
- ☐ Passport
- ☐ Other:

I.D. Number:

Issued By:

Issued Date:

Expiration Date:

Document Type:

Date/Time Notarized: **AM PM**

Document Date:

Fee Charged:

Printed Name and Address of Witness:

1.

2.

Witness' Signature:

1.

2.

Comments :

Record Number:

NOTARY RECORD

Printed Name and Address of Signer:

Phone Number:

Email:

Signer's Signature:

Thumb Print:

Service Performed:

- ☐ Oath
- ☐ Acknowledgment
- ☐ Jurat
- ☐ Other:

Identification:

- ☐ I.D Card
- ☐ Credible Witness
- ☐ Drivers License
- ☐ Known Personally
- ☐ Passport
- ☐ Other:

I.D. Number:

Issued By:

Issued Date:

Expiration Date:

Document Type:

Date/Time Notarized: **AM PM**

Document Date:

Fee Charged:

Printed Name and Address of Witness:

1.

2.

Witness' Signature:

1.

2

Comments :

Record Number:

NOTARY RECORD

Printed Name and Address of Signer:	Phone Number:	Thumb Print:
	Email:	
	Signer's Signature:	

Service Performed:	Identification:		I.D. Number:	
☐ Oath	☐ I.D Card	☐ Credible Witness		
☐ Acknowledgment	☐ Drivers License	☐ Known Personally	Issued By:	
☐ Jurat	☐ Passport			
☐ Other:	☐ Other:		Issued Date:	Expiration Date:
Document Type:	Date/Time Notarized: AM PM		Document Date:	Fee Charged:

Printed Name and Address of Witness:	Witness' Signature:
1.	1.
2.	2.

Comments :	Record Number:

NOTARY RECORD

Printed Name and Address of Signer:	Phone Number:	Thumb Print:
	Email:	
	Signer's Signature:	

Service Performed:	Identification:		I.D. Number:	
☐ Oath	☐ I.D Card	☐ Credible Witness		
☐ Acknowledgment	☐ Drivers License	☐ Known Personally	Issued By:	
☐ Jurat	☐ Passport			
☐ Other:	☐ Other:		Issued Date:	Expiration Date:
Document Type:	Date/Time Notarized: AM PM		Document Date:	Fee Charged:

Printed Name and Address of Witness:	Witness' Signature:
1.	1.
2.	2

Comments :	Record Number:

NOTARY RECORD

Printed Name and Address of Signer:	Phone Number:	Thumb Print:
	Email:	
	Signer's Signature:	

Service Performed:	Identification:		I.D. Number:	
☐ Oath	☐ I.D Card	☐ Credible Witness	Issued By:	
☐ Acknowledgment	☐ Drivers License	☐ Known Personally	Issued Date:	Expiration Date:
☐ Jurat	☐ Passport			
☐ Other:	☐ Other:			
Document Type:	Date/Time Notarized: AM PM		Document Date:	Fee Charged:

Printed Name and Address of Witness:	Witness' Signature:
1.	1.
2.	2.

Comments :	Record Number:

NOTARY RECORD

Printed Name and Address of Signer:	Phone Number:	Thumb Print:
	Email:	
	Signer's Signature:	

Service Performed:	Identification:		I.D. Number:	
☐ Oath	☐ I.D Card	☐ Credible Witness	Issued By:	
☐ Acknowledgment	☐ Drivers License	☐ Known Personally	Issued Date:	Expiration Date:
☐ Jurat	☐ Passport			
☐ Other:	☐ Other:			
Document Type:	Date/Time Notarized: AM PM		Document Date:	Fee Charged:

Printed Name and Address of Witness:	Witness' Signature:
1.	1.
2.	2

Comments :	Record Number:

NOTARY RECORD

Printed Name and Address of Signer:	Phone Number:	Thumb Print:
	Email:	
	Signer's Signature:	

Service Performed:	Identification:		I.D. Number:	
☐ Oath	☐ I.D Card	☐ Credible Witness		
☐ Acknowledgment	☐ Drivers License	☐ Known Personally	Issued By:	
☐ Jurat	☐ Passport			
☐ Other:	☐ Other:		Issued Date:	Expiration Date:
Document Type:	Date/Time Notarized: AM PM		Document Date:	Fee Charged:

Printed Name and Address of Witness:	Witness' Signature:
1.	1.
2.	2.

Comments :	Record Number:

NOTARY RECORD

Printed Name and Address of Signer:	Phone Number:	Thumb Print:
	Email:	
	Signer's Signature:	

Service Performed:	Identification:		I.D. Number:	
☐ Oath	☐ I.D Card	☐ Credible Witness		
☐ Acknowledgment	☐ Drivers License	☐ Known Personally	Issued By:	
☐ Jurat	☐ Passport			
☐ Other:	☐ Other:		Issued Date:	Expiration Date:
Document Type:	Date/Time Notarized: AM PM		Document Date:	Fee Charged:

Printed Name and Address of Witness:	Witness' Signature:
1.	1.
2.	2

Comments :	Record Number:

NOTARY RECORD

Printed Name and Address of Signer:	Phone Number:	Thumb Print:
	Email:	
	Signer's Signature:	

Service Performed:	Identification:		I.D. Number:	
☐ Oath	☐ I.D Card	☐ Credible Witness	Issued By:	
☐ Acknowledgment	☐ Drivers License	☐ Known Personally		
☐ Jurat	☐ Passport		Issued Date:	Expiration Date:
☐ Other:	☐ Other:			
Document Type:	Date/Time Notarized: AM PM		Document Date:	Fee Charged:

Printed Name and Address of Witness:	Witness' Signature:
1.	1.
2.	2.

Comments :	Record Number:

NOTARY RECORD

Printed Name and Address of Signer:	Phone Number:	Thumb Print:
	Email:	
	Signer's Signature:	

Service Performed:	Identification:		I.D. Number:	
☐ Oath	☐ I.D Card	☐ Credible Witness	Issued By:	
☐ Acknowledgment	☐ Drivers License	☐ Known Personally		
☐ Jurat	☐ Passport		Issued Date:	Expiration Date:
☐ Other:	☐ Other:			
Document Type:	Date/Time Notarized: AM PM		Document Date:	Fee Charged:

Printed Name and Address of Witness:	Witness' Signature:
1.	1.
2.	2

Comments :	Record Number:

NOTARY RECORD

Printed Name and Address of Signer:

Phone Number:

Email:

Signer's Signature:

Thumb Print:

Service Performed:

- ☐ Oath
- ☐ Acknowledgment
- ☐ Jurat
- ☐ Other:

Identification:

- ☐ I.D Card
- ☐ Credible Witness
- ☐ Drivers License
- ☐ Known Personally
- ☐ Passport
- ☐ Other:

I.D. Number:

Issued By:

Issued Date:

Expiration Date:

Document Type:

Date/Time Notarized: AM PM

Document Date:

Fee Charged:

Printed Name and Address of Witness:

1.

2.

Witness' Signature:

1.

2.

Comments :

Record Number:

NOTARY RECORD

Printed Name and Address of Signer:

Phone Number:

Email:

Signer's Signature:

Thumb Print:

Service Performed:

- ☐ Oath
- ☐ Acknowledgment
- ☐ Jurat
- ☐ Other:

Identification:

- ☐ I.D Card
- ☐ Credible Witness
- ☐ Drivers License
- ☐ Known Personally
- ☐ Passport
- ☐ Other:

I.D. Number:

Issued By:

Issued Date:

Expiration Date:

Document Type:

Date/Time Notarized: AM PM

Document Date:

Fee Charged:

Printed Name and Address of Witness:

1.

2.

Witness' Signature:

1.

2

Comments :

Record Number:

NOTARY RECORD

Printed Name and Address of Signer:	**Phone Number:**	**Thumb Print:**
	Email:	
	Signer's Signature:	

Service Performed: ☐ Oath ☐ Acknowledgment ☐ Jurat ☐ Other:	**Identification:** ☐ I.D Card ☐ Credible Witness ☐ Drivers License ☐ Known Personally ☐ Passport ☐ Other:	**I.D. Number:**	
		Issued By:	
		Issued Date:	**Expiration Date:**
Document Type:	**Date/Time Notarized:** **AM** **PM**	**Document Date:**	**Fee Charged:**

Printed Name and Address of Witness: **1.** **2.**	**Witness' Signature:** **1.** **2.**
Comments :	**Record Number:**

NOTARY RECORD

Printed Name and Address of Signer:	**Phone Number:**	**Thumb Print:**
	Email:	
	Signer's Signature:	

Service Performed: ☐ Oath ☐ Acknowledgment ☐ Jurat ☐ Other:	**Identification:** ☐ I.D Card ☐ Credible Witness ☐ Drivers License ☐ Known Personally ☐ Passport ☐ Other:	**I.D. Number:**	
		Issued By:	
		Issued Date:	**Expiration Date:**
Document Type:	**Date/Time Notarized:** **AM** **PM**	**Document Date:**	**Fee Charged:**

Printed Name and Address of Witness: **1.** **2.**	**Witness' Signature:** **1.** **2**
Comments :	**Record Number:**

NOTARY RECORD

Printed Name and Address of Signer:	Phone Number:	Thumb Print:
	Email:	
	Signer's Signature:	

Service Performed:	Identification:		I.D. Number:	
☐ Oath	☐ I.D Card	☐ Credible Witness	Issued By:	
☐ Acknowledgment	☐ Drivers License	☐ Known Personally		
☐ Jurat	☐ Passport		Issued Date:	Expiration Date:
☐ Other:	☐ Other:			
Document Type:	Date/Time Notarized:	AM PM	Document Date:	Fee Charged:

Printed Name and Address of Witness:	Witness' Signature:
1.	1.
2.	2.

Comments :	Record Number:

NOTARY RECORD

Printed Name and Address of Signer:	Phone Number:	Thumb Print:
	Email:	
	Signer's Signature:	

Service Performed:	Identification:		I.D. Number:	
☐ Oath	☐ I.D Card	☐ Credible Witness	Issued By:	
☐ Acknowledgment	☐ Drivers License	☐ Known Personally		
☐ Jurat	☐ Passport		Issued Date:	Expiration Date:
☐ Other:	☐ Other:			
Document Type:	Date/Time Notarized:	AM PM	Document Date:	Fee Charged:

Printed Name and Address of Witness:	Witness' Signature:
1.	1.
2.	2

Comments :	Record Number:

NOTARY RECORD

Printed Name and Address of Signer:	Phone Number:	Thumb Print:
	Email:	
	Signer's Signature:	

Service Performed:	Identification:		I.D. Number:	
☐ Oath	☐ I.D Card	☐ Credible Witness		
☐ Acknowledgment	☐ Drivers License	☐ Known Personally	Issued By:	
☐ Jurat	☐ Passport			
☐ Other:	☐ Other:		Issued Date:	Expiration Date:
Document Type:	Date/Time Notarized: AM PM		Document Date:	Fee Charged:

Printed Name and Address of Witness:	Witness' Signature:
1.	1.
2.	2.

Comments :	Record Number:

NOTARY RECORD

Printed Name and Address of Signer:	Phone Number:	Thumb Print:
	Email:	
	Signer's Signature:	

Service Performed:	Identification:		I.D. Number:	
☐ Oath	☐ I.D Card	☐ Credible Witness		
☐ Acknowledgment	☐ Drivers License	☐ Known Personally	Issued By:	
☐ Jurat	☐ Passport			
☐ Other:	☐ Other:		Issued Date:	Expiration Date:
Document Type:	Date/Time Notarized: AM PM		Document Date:	Fee Charged:

Printed Name and Address of Witness:	Witness' Signature:
1.	1.
2.	2

Comments :	Record Number:

NOTARY RECORD

Printed Name and Address of Signer:	**Phone Number:**	**Thumb Print:**
	Email:	
	Signer's Signature:	

Service Performed: ☐ Oath ☐ Acknowledgment ☐ Jurat ☐ Other:	**Identification:** ☐ I.D Card ☐ Credible Witness ☐ Drivers License ☐ Known Personally ☐ Passport ☐ Other:	**I.D. Number:**	
		Issued By:	
		Issued Date:	**Expiration Date:**
Document Type:	**Date/Time Notarized:** AM PM	**Document Date:**	**Fee Charged:**

Printed Name and Address of Witness: **1.** **2.**	**Witness' Signature:** **1.** **2.**

Comments :	**Record Number:**

NOTARY RECORD

Printed Name and Address of Signer:	**Phone Number:**	**Thumb Print:**
	Email:	
	Signer's Signature:	

Service Performed: ☐ Oath ☐ Acknowledgment ☐ Jurat ☐ Other:	**Identification:** ☐ I.D Card ☐ Credible Witness ☐ Drivers License ☐ Known Personally ☐ Passport ☐ Other:	**I.D. Number:**	
		Issued By:	
		Issued Date:	**Expiration Date:**
Document Type:	**Date/Time Notarized:** AM PM	**Document Date:**	**Fee Charged:**

Printed Name and Address of Witness: **1.** **2.**	**Witness' Signature:** **1.** **2**

Comments :	**Record Number:**

NOTARY RECORD

Printed Name and Address of Signer:	Phone Number:	Thumb Print:
	Email:	
	Signer's Signature:	

Service Performed:	Identification:		I.D. Number:	
☐ Oath	☐ I.D Card	☐ Credible Witness	Issued By:	
☐ Acknowledgment	☐ Drivers License	☐ Known Personally		
☐ Jurat	☐ Passport		Issued Date:	Expiration Date:
☐ Other:	☐ Other:			
Document Type:	Date/Time Notarized: AM PM		Document Date:	Fee Charged:

Printed Name and Address of Witness:	Witness' Signature:
1.	1.
2.	2.

Comments :	Record Number:

NOTARY RECORD

Printed Name and Address of Signer:	Phone Number:	Thumb Print:
	Email:	
	Signer's Signature:	

Service Performed:	Identification:		I.D. Number:	
☐ Oath	☐ I.D Card	☐ Credible Witness	Issued By:	
☐ Acknowledgment	☐ Drivers License	☐ Known Personally		
☐ Jurat	☐ Passport		Issued Date:	Expiration Date:
☐ Other:	☐ Other:			
Document Type:	Date/Time Notarized: AM PM		Document Date:	Fee Charged:

Printed Name and Address of Witness:	Witness' Signature:
1.	1.
2.	2

Comments :	Record Number:

NOTARY RECORD

Printed Name and Address of Signer:	Phone Number:	Thumb Print:
	Email:	
	Signer's Signature:	

Service Performed:	Identification:		I.D. Number:	
☐ Oath	☐ I.D Card	☐ Credible Witness	Issued By:	
☐ Acknowledgment	☐ Drivers License	☐ Known Personally	Issued Date:	Expiration Date:
☐ Jurat	☐ Passport			
☐ Other:	☐ Other:			
Document Type:	Date/Time Notarized: AM PM		Document Date:	Fee Charged:

Printed Name and Address of Witness:	Witness' Signature:
1.	1.
2.	2.

Comments :	Record Number:

NOTARY RECORD

Printed Name and Address of Signer:	Phone Number:	Thumb Print:
	Email:	
	Signer's Signature:	

Service Performed:	Identification:		I.D. Number:	
☐ Oath	☐ I.D Card	☐ Credible Witness	Issued By:	
☐ Acknowledgment	☐ Drivers License	☐ Known Personally	Issued Date:	Expiration Date:
☐ Jurat	☐ Passport			
☐ Other:	☐ Other:			
Document Type:	Date/Time Notarized: AM PM		Document Date:	Fee Charged:

Printed Name and Address of Witness:	Witness' Signature:
1.	1.
2.	2

Comments :	Record Number:

NOTARY RECORD

Printed Name and Address of Signer:

Phone Number:

Email:

Signer's Signature:

Thumb Print:

Service Performed:

- ☐ Oath
- ☐ Acknowledgment
- ☐ Jurat
- ☐ Other:

Identification:

- ☐ I.D Card
- ☐ Credible Witness
- ☐ Drivers License
- ☐ Known Personally
- ☐ Passport
- ☐ Other:

I.D. Number:

Issued By:

Issued Date:

Expiration Date:

Document Type:

Date/Time Notarized: **AM** **PM**

Document Date:

Fee Charged:

Printed Name and Address of Witness:

1.

2.

Witness' Signature:

1.

2.

Comments :

Record Number:

NOTARY RECORD

Printed Name and Address of Signer:

Phone Number:

Email:

Signer's Signature:

Thumb Print:

Service Performed:

- ☐ Oath
- ☐ Acknowledgment
- ☐ Jurat
- ☐ Other:

Identification:

- ☐ I.D Card
- ☐ Credible Witness
- ☐ Drivers License
- ☐ Known Personally
- ☐ Passport
- ☐ Other:

I.D. Number:

Issued By:

Issued Date:

Expiration Date:

Document Type:

Date/Time Notarized: **AM** **PM**

Document Date:

Fee Charged:

Printed Name and Address of Witness:

1.

2.

Witness' Signature:

1.

2

Comments :

Record Number:

NOTARY RECORD

Printed Name and Address of Signer:	**Phone Number:**	**Thumb Print:**
	Email:	
	Signer's Signature:	

Service Performed: ☐ Oath ☐ Acknowledgment ☐ Jurat ☐ Other:	**Identification:** ☐ I.D Card ☐ Credible Witness ☐ Drivers License ☐ Known Personally ☐ Passport ☐ Other:	**I.D. Number:**	
		Issued By:	
		Issued Date:	**Expiration Date:**
Document Type:	**Date/Time Notarized:** AM PM	**Document Date:**	**Fee Charged:**

Printed Name and Address of Witness: **1.** **2.**	**Witness' Signature:** **1.** **2.**
Comments :	**Record Number:**

NOTARY RECORD

Printed Name and Address of Signer:	**Phone Number:**	**Thumb Print:**
	Email:	
	Signer's Signature:	

Service Performed: ☐ Oath ☐ Acknowledgment ☐ Jurat ☐ Other:	**Identification:** ☐ I.D Card ☐ Credible Witness ☐ Drivers License ☐ Known Personally ☐ Passport ☐ Other:	**I.D. Number:**	
		Issued By:	
		Issued Date:	**Expiration Date:**
Document Type:	**Date/Time Notarized:** AM PM	**Document Date:**	**Fee Charged:**

Printed Name and Address of Witness: **1.** **2.**	**Witness' Signature:** **1.** **2**
Comments :	**Record Number:**

NOTARY RECORD

Printed Name and Address of Signer:	Phone Number:	Thumb Print:
	Email:	
	Signer's Signature:	

Service Performed:	Identification:		I.D. Number:	
☐ Oath	☐ I.D Card	☐ Credible Witness		
☐ Acknowledgment	☐ Drivers License	☐ Known Personally	Issued By:	
☐ Jurat	☐ Passport			
☐ Other:	☐ Other:		Issued Date:	Expiration Date:
Document Type:	Date/Time Notarized: AM PM		Document Date:	Fee Charged:

Printed Name and Address of Witness:	Witness' Signature:
1.	1.
2.	2.

Comments :	Record Number:

NOTARY RECORD

Printed Name and Address of Signer:	Phone Number:	Thumb Print:
	Email:	
	Signer's Signature:	

Service Performed:	Identification:		I.D. Number:	
☐ Oath	☐ I.D Card	☐ Credible Witness		
☐ Acknowledgment	☐ Drivers License	☐ Known Personally	Issued By:	
☐ Jurat	☐ Passport			
☐ Other:	☐ Other:		Issued Date:	Expiration Date:
Document Type:	Date/Time Notarized: AM PM		Document Date:	Fee Charged:

Printed Name and Address of Witness:	Witness' Signature:
1.	1.
2.	2

Comments :	Record Number:

NOTARY RECORD

Printed Name and Address of Signer:	Phone Number:	Thumb Print:
	Email:	
	Signer's Signature:	

Service Performed:	Identification:		I.D. Number:	
☐ Oath	☐ I.D Card	☐ Credible Witness		
☐ Acknowledgment	☐ Drivers License	☐ Known Personally	Issued By:	
☐ Jurat	☐ Passport			
☐ Other:	☐ Other:		Issued Date:	Expiration Date:
Document Type:	Date/Time Notarized: AM PM		Document Date:	Fee Charged:

Printed Name and Address of Witness:	Witness' Signature:
1.	1.
2.	2.

Comments :	Record Number:

NOTARY RECORD

Printed Name and Address of Signer:	Phone Number:	Thumb Print:
	Email:	
	Signer's Signature:	

Service Performed:	Identification:		I.D. Number:	
☐ Oath	☐ I.D Card	☐ Credible Witness		
☐ Acknowledgment	☐ Drivers License	☐ Known Personally	Issued By:	
☐ Jurat	☐ Passport			
☐ Other:	☐ Other:		Issued Date:	Expiration Date:
Document Type:	Date/Time Notarized: AM PM		Document Date:	Fee Charged:

Printed Name and Address of Witness:	Witness' Signature:
1.	1.
2.	2

Comments :	Record Number:

NOTARY RECORD

Printed Name and Address of Signer:	Phone Number:	Thumb Print:
	Email:	
	Signer's Signature:	

Service Performed:	Identification:		I.D. Number:	
☐ Oath	☐ I.D Card	☐ Credible Witness		
☐ Acknowledgment	☐ Drivers License	☐ Known Personally	Issued By:	
☐ Jurat	☐ Passport			
☐ Other:	☐ Other:		Issued Date:	Expiration Date:
Document Type:	Date/Time Notarized:	AM PM	Document Date:	Fee Charged:

Printed Name and Address of Witness:	Witness' Signature:
1.	1.
2.	2.

Comments :	Record Number:

NOTARY RECORD

Printed Name and Address of Signer:	Phone Number:	Thumb Print:
	Email:	
	Signer's Signature:	

Service Performed:	Identification:		I.D. Number:	
☐ Oath	☐ I.D Card	☐ Credible Witness		
☐ Acknowledgment	☐ Drivers License	☐ Known Personally	Issued By:	
☐ Jurat	☐ Passport			
☐ Other:	☐ Other:		Issued Date:	Expiration Date:
Document Type:	Date/Time Notarized:	AM PM	Document Date:	Fee Charged:

Printed Name and Address of Witness:	Witness' Signature:
1.	1.
2.	2

Comments :	Record Number:

NOTARY RECORD

Printed Name and Address of Signer:	**Phone Number:**	**Thumb Print:**
	Email:	
	Signer's Signature:	

Service Performed: ☐ Oath ☐ Acknowledgment ☐ Jurat ☐ Other:	**Identification:** ☐ I.D Card ☐ Credible Witness ☐ Drivers License ☐ Known Personally ☐ Passport ☐ Other:	**I.D. Number:**	
		Issued By:	
		Issued Date:	**Expiration Date:**
Document Type:	**Date/Time Notarized:** AM PM	**Document Date:**	**Fee Charged:**

Printed Name and Address of Witness: **1.** **2.**	**Witness' Signature:** **1.** **2.**
Comments :	**Record Number:**

NOTARY RECORD

Printed Name and Address of Signer:	**Phone Number:**	**Thumb Print:**
	Email:	
	Signer's Signature:	

Service Performed: ☐ Oath ☐ Acknowledgment ☐ Jurat ☐ Other:	**Identification:** ☐ I.D Card ☐ Credible Witness ☐ Drivers License ☐ Known Personally ☐ Passport ☐ Other:	**I.D. Number:**	
		Issued By:	
		Issued Date:	**Expiration Date:**
Document Type:	**Date/Time Notarized:** AM PM	**Document Date:**	**Fee Charged:**

Printed Name and Address of Witness: **1.** **2.**	**Witness' Signature:** **1.** **2**
Comments :	**Record Number:**

NOTARY RECORD

Printed Name and Address of Signer:	**Phone Number:** **Email:** **Signer's Signature:**	**Thumb Print:**

Service Performed: ☐ Oath ☐ Acknowledgment ☐ Jurat ☐ Other:	**Identification:** ☐ I.D Card ☐ Credible Witness ☐ Drivers License ☐ Known Personally ☐ Passport ☐ Other:	**I.D. Number:** **Issued By:** **Issued Date:**	**Expiration Date:**
Document Type:	**Date/Time Notarized:** AM PM	**Document Date:**	**Fee Charged:**

Printed Name and Address of Witness: **1.** **2.**	**Witness' Signature:** **1.** **2.**
Comments :	**Record Number:**

NOTARY RECORD

Printed Name and Address of Signer:	**Phone Number:** **Email:** **Signer's Signature:**	**Thumb Print:**

Service Performed: ☐ Oath ☐ Acknowledgment ☐ Jurat ☐ Other:	**Identification:** ☐ I.D Card ☐ Credible Witness ☐ Drivers License ☐ Known Personally ☐ Passport ☐ Other:	**I.D. Number:** **Issued By:** **Issued Date:**	**Expiration Date:**
Document Type:	**Date/Time Notarized:** AM PM	**Document Date:**	**Fee Charged:**

Printed Name and Address of Witness: **1.** **2.**	**Witness' Signature:** **1.** **2**
Comments :	**Record Number:**

NOTARY RECORD

Printed Name and Address of Signer:	Phone Number:	Thumb Print:
	Email:	
	Signer's Signature:	

Service Performed:	Identification:		I.D. Number:	
☐ Oath	☐ I.D Card	☐ Credible Witness	Issued By:	
☐ Acknowledgment	☐ Drivers License	☐ Known Personally		
☐ Jurat	☐ Passport		Issued Date:	Expiration Date:
☐ Other:	☐ Other:			
Document Type:	Date/Time Notarized: AM PM		Document Date:	Fee Charged:

Printed Name and Address of Witness:	Witness' Signature:
1.	1.
2.	2.
Comments :	Record Number:

NOTARY RECORD

Printed Name and Address of Signer:	Phone Number:	Thumb Print:
	Email:	
	Signer's Signature:	

Service Performed:	Identification:		I.D. Number:	
☐ Oath	☐ I.D Card	☐ Credible Witness	Issued By:	
☐ Acknowledgment	☐ Drivers License	☐ Known Personally		
☐ Jurat	☐ Passport		Issued Date:	Expiration Date:
☐ Other:	☐ Other:			
Document Type:	Date/Time Notarized: AM PM		Document Date:	Fee Charged:

Printed Name and Address of Witness:	Witness' Signature:
1.	1.
2.	2
Comments :	Record Number:

NOTARY RECORD

Printed Name and Address of Signer:	Phone Number:	Thumb Print:
	Email:	
	Signer's Signature:	

Service Performed:	Identification:		I.D. Number:	
☐ Oath	☐ I.D Card	☐ Credible Witness	Issued By:	
☐ Acknowledgment	☐ Drivers License	☐ Known Personally		
☐ Jurat	☐ Passport		Issued Date:	Expiration Date:
☐ Other:	☐ Other:			
Document Type:	Date/Time Notarized: AM PM		Document Date:	Fee Charged:

Printed Name and Address of Witness:	Witness' Signature:
1.	1.
2.	2.

Comments :	Record Number:

NOTARY RECORD

Printed Name and Address of Signer:	Phone Number:	Thumb Print:
	Email:	
	Signer's Signature:	

Service Performed:	Identification:		I.D. Number:	
☐ Oath	☐ I.D Card	☐ Credible Witness	Issued By:	
☐ Acknowledgment	☐ Drivers License	☐ Known Personally		
☐ Jurat	☐ Passport		Issued Date:	Expiration Date:
☐ Other:	☐ Other:			
Document Type:	Date/Time Notarized: AM PM		Document Date:	Fee Charged:

Printed Name and Address of Witness:	Witness' Signature:
1.	1.
2.	2

Comments :	Record Number:

NOTARY RECORD

Printed Name and Address of Signer:	Phone Number:	Thumb Print:
	Email:	
	Signer's Signature:	

Service Performed:	Identification:		I.D. Number:	
☐ Oath	☐ I.D Card	☐ Credible Witness	Issued By:	
☐ Acknowledgment	☐ Drivers License	☐ Known Personally	Issued Date:	Expiration Date:
☐ Jurat	☐ Passport			
☐ Other:	☐ Other:			
Document Type:	Date/Time Notarized:	AM PM	Document Date:	Fee Charged:

Printed Name and Address of Witness:	Witness' Signature:
1.	1.
2.	2.

Comments :	Record Number:

NOTARY RECORD

Printed Name and Address of Signer:	Phone Number:	Thumb Print:
	Email:	
	Signer's Signature:	

Service Performed:	Identification:		I.D. Number:	
☐ Oath	☐ I.D Card	☐ Credible Witness	Issued By:	
☐ Acknowledgment	☐ Drivers License	☐ Known Personally	Issued Date:	Expiration Date:
☐ Jurat	☐ Passport			
☐ Other:	☐ Other:			
Document Type:	Date/Time Notarized:	AM PM	Document Date:	Fee Charged:

Printed Name and Address of Witness:	Witness' Signature:
1.	1.
2.	2

Comments :	Record Number:

NOTARY RECORD

Printed Name and Address of Signer:	**Phone Number:** **Email:** **Signer's Signature:**	**Thumb Print:**

Service Performed: ☐ Oath ☐ Acknowledgment ☐ Jurat ☐ Other:	**Identification:** ☐ I.D Card ☐ Credible Witness ☐ Drivers License ☐ Known Personally ☐ Passport ☐ Other:	**I.D. Number:** **Issued By:** **Issued Date:**	**Expiration Date:**
Document Type:	**Date/Time Notarized:** AM PM	**Document Date:**	**Fee Charged:**

Printed Name and Address of Witness: **1.** **2.**	**Witness' Signature:** **1.** **2.**
Comments :	**Record Number:**

NOTARY RECORD

Printed Name and Address of Signer:	**Phone Number:** **Email:** **Signer's Signature:**	**Thumb Print:**

Service Performed: ☐ Oath ☐ Acknowledgment ☐ Jurat ☐ Other:	**Identification:** ☐ I.D Card ☐ Credible Witness ☐ Drivers License ☐ Known Personally ☐ Passport ☐ Other:	**I.D. Number:** **Issued By:** **Issued Date:**	**Expiration Date:**
Document Type:	**Date/Time Notarized:** AM PM	**Document Date:**	**Fee Charged:**

Printed Name and Address of Witness: **1.** **2.**	**Witness' Signature:** **1.** **2**
Comments :	**Record Number:**

NOTARY RECORD

Printed Name and Address of Signer:	**Phone Number:**	**Thumb Print:**
	Email:	
	Signer's Signature:	

Service Performed: ☐ Oath ☐ Acknowledgment ☐ Jurat ☐ Other:	**Identification:** ☐ I.D Card ☐ Credible Witness ☐ Drivers License ☐ Known Personally ☐ Passport ☐ Other:	**I.D. Number:**	
		Issued By:	
		Issued Date:	**Expiration Date:**
Document Type:	**Date/Time Notarized:** AM PM	**Document Date:**	**Fee Charged:**

Printed Name and Address of Witness: **1.** **2.**	**Witness' Signature:** **1.** **2.**
Comments :	**Record Number:**

NOTARY RECORD

Printed Name and Address of Signer:	**Phone Number:**	**Thumb Print:**
	Email:	
	Signer's Signature:	

Service Performed: ☐ Oath ☐ Acknowledgment ☐ Jurat ☐ Other:	**Identification:** ☐ I.D Card ☐ Credible Witness ☐ Drivers License ☐ Known Personally ☐ Passport ☐ Other:	**I.D. Number:**	
		Issued By:	
		Issued Date:	**Expiration Date:**
Document Type:	**Date/Time Notarized:** AM PM	**Document Date:**	**Fee Charged:**

Printed Name and Address of Witness: **1.** **2.**	**Witness' Signature:** **1.** **2**
Comments :	**Record Number:**

NOTARY RECORD

Printed Name and Address of Signer:	**Phone Number:**	**Thumb Print:**
	Email:	
	Signer's Signature:	

Service Performed: ☐ Oath ☐ Acknowledgment ☐ Jurat ☐ Other:	**Identification:** ☐ I.D Card ☐ Credible Witness ☐ Drivers License ☐ Known Personally ☐ Passport ☐ Other:	**I.D. Number:**	
		Issued By:	
		Issued Date:	**Expiration Date:**
Document Type:	**Date/Time Notarized:** **AM** **PM**	**Document Date:**	**Fee Charged:**

Printed Name and Address of Witness: **1.** **2.**	**Witness' Signature:** **1.** **2.**
Comments :	**Record Number:**

NOTARY RECORD

Printed Name and Address of Signer:	**Phone Number:**	**Thumb Print:**
	Email:	
	Signer's Signature:	

Service Performed: ☐ Oath ☐ Acknowledgment ☐ Jurat ☐ Other:	**Identification:** ☐ I.D Card ☐ Credible Witness ☐ Drivers License ☐ Known Personally ☐ Passport ☐ Other:	**I.D. Number:**	
		Issued By:	
		Issued Date:	**Expiration Date:**
Document Type:	**Date/Time Notarized:** **AM** **PM**	**Document Date:**	**Fee Charged:**

Printed Name and Address of Witness: **1.** **2.**	**Witness' Signature:** **1.** **2**
Comments :	**Record Number:**

NOTARY RECORD

Printed Name and Address of Signer:	Phone Number:	Thumb Print:
	Email:	
	Signer's Signature:	

Service Performed:	Identification:		I.D. Number:	
☐ Oath	☐ I.D Card	☐ Credible Witness	Issued By:	
☐ Acknowledgment	☐ Drivers License	☐ Known Personally		
☐ Jurat	☐ Passport		Issued Date:	Expiration Date:
☐ Other:	☐ Other:			
Document Type:	Date/Time Notarized:	AM PM	Document Date:	Fee Charged:

Printed Name and Address of Witness:	Witness' Signature:
1.	1.
2.	2.

Comments :	Record Number:

NOTARY RECORD

Printed Name and Address of Signer:	Phone Number:	Thumb Print:
	Email:	
	Signer's Signature:	

Service Performed:	Identification:		I.D. Number:	
☐ Oath	☐ I.D Card	☐ Credible Witness	Issued By:	
☐ Acknowledgment	☐ Drivers License	☐ Known Personally		
☐ Jurat	☐ Passport		Issued Date:	Expiration Date:
☐ Other:	☐ Other:			
Document Type:	Date/Time Notarized:	AM PM	Document Date:	Fee Charged:

Printed Name and Address of Witness:	Witness' Signature:
1.	1.
2.	2

Comments :	Record Number:

NOTARY RECORD

Printed Name and Address of Signer:	**Phone Number:**	**Thumb Print:**
	Email:	
	Signer's Signature:	

Service Performed:	**Identification:**		**I.D. Number:**	
☐ Oath	☐ I.D Card	☐ Credible Witness		
☐ Acknowledgment	☐ Drivers License	☐ Known Personally	**Issued By:**	
☐ Jurat	☐ Passport			
☐ Other:	☐ Other:		**Issued Date:**	**Expiration Date:**
Document Type:	**Date/Time Notarized:**	AM PM	**Document Date:**	**Fee Charged:**

Printed Name and Address of Witness:	**Witness' Signature:**
1.	**1.**
2.	**2.**

Comments :	**Record Number:**

NOTARY RECORD

Printed Name and Address of Signer:	**Phone Number:**	**Thumb Print:**
	Email:	
	Signer's Signature:	

Service Performed:	**Identification:**		**I.D. Number:**	
☐ Oath	☐ I.D Card	☐ Credible Witness		
☐ Acknowledgment	☐ Drivers License	☐ Known Personally	**Issued By:**	
☐ Jurat	☐ Passport			
☐ Other:	☐ Other:		**Issued Date:**	**Expiration Date:**
Document Type:	**Date/Time Notarized:**	AM PM	**Document Date:**	**Fee Charged:**

Printed Name and Address of Witness:	**Witness' Signature:**
1.	**1.**
2.	**2**

Comments :	**Record Number:**

NOTARY RECORD

Printed Name and Address of Signer:	**Phone Number:**	**Thumb Print:**
	Email:	
	Signer's Signature:	

Service Performed: ☐ Oath ☐ Acknowledgment ☐ Jurat ☐ Other:	**Identification:** ☐ I.D Card ☐ Credible Witness ☐ Drivers License ☐ Known Personally ☐ Passport ☐ Other:	**I.D. Number:**	
		Issued By:	
		Issued Date:	**Expiration Date:**
Document Type:	**Date/Time Notarized:** AM PM	**Document Date:**	**Fee Charged:**

Printed Name and Address of Witness: **1.** **2.**	**Witness' Signature:** **1.** **2.**
Comments :	**Record Number:**

NOTARY RECORD

Printed Name and Address of Signer:	**Phone Number:**	**Thumb Print:**
	Email:	
	Signer's Signature:	

Service Performed: ☐ Oath ☐ Acknowledgment ☐ Jurat ☐ Other:	**Identification:** ☐ I.D Card ☐ Credible Witness ☐ Drivers License ☐ Known Personally ☐ Passport ☐ Other:	**I.D. Number:**	
		Issued By:	
		Issued Date:	**Expiration Date:**
Document Type:	**Date/Time Notarized:** AM PM	**Document Date:**	**Fee Charged:**

Printed Name and Address of Witness: **1.** **2.**	**Witness' Signature:** **1.** **2**
Comments :	**Record Number:**

NOTARY RECORD

Printed Name and Address of Signer:	Phone Number:	Thumb Print:
	Email:	
	Signer's Signature:	

Service Performed:	Identification:		I.D. Number:	
☐ Oath	☐ I.D Card	☐ Credible Witness		
☐ Acknowledgment	☐ Drivers License	☐ Known Personally	Issued By:	
☐ Jurat	☐ Passport			
☐ Other:	☐ Other:		Issued Date:	Expiration Date:
Document Type:	Date/Time Notarized: AM PM		Document Date:	Fee Charged:

Printed Name and Address of Witness:	Witness' Signature:
1.	1.
2.	2.

Comments :	Record Number:

NOTARY RECORD

Printed Name and Address of Signer:	Phone Number:	Thumb Print:
	Email:	
	Signer's Signature:	

Service Performed:	Identification:		I.D. Number:	
☐ Oath	☐ I.D Card	☐ Credible Witness		
☐ Acknowledgment	☐ Drivers License	☐ Known Personally	Issued By:	
☐ Jurat	☐ Passport			
☐ Other:	☐ Other:		Issued Date:	Expiration Date:
Document Type:	Date/Time Notarized: AM PM		Document Date:	Fee Charged:

Printed Name and Address of Witness:	Witness' Signature:
1.	1.
2.	2

Comments :	Record Number:

NOTARY RECORD

Printed Name and Address of Signer:	Phone Number:	Thumb Print:
	Email:	
	Signer's Signature:	

Service Performed:	Identification:		I.D. Number:	
☐ Oath	☐ I.D Card	☐ Credible Witness	Issued By:	
☐ Acknowledgment	☐ Drivers License	☐ Known Personally		
☐ Jurat	☐ Passport		Issued Date:	Expiration Date:
☐ Other:	☐ Other:			
Document Type:	Date/Time Notarized: AM PM		Document Date:	Fee Charged:

Printed Name and Address of Witness:	Witness' Signature:
1.	1.
2.	2.

Comments :	Record Number:

NOTARY RECORD

Printed Name and Address of Signer:	Phone Number:	Thumb Print:
	Email:	
	Signer's Signature:	

Service Performed:	Identification:		I.D. Number:	
☐ Oath	☐ I.D Card	☐ Credible Witness	Issued By:	
☐ Acknowledgment	☐ Drivers License	☐ Known Personally		
☐ Jurat	☐ Passport		Issued Date:	Expiration Date:
☐ Other:	☐ Other:			
Document Type:	Date/Time Notarized: AM PM		Document Date:	Fee Charged:

Printed Name and Address of Witness:	Witness' Signature:
1.	1.
2.	2

Comments :	Record Number:

NOTARY RECORD

Printed Name and Address of Signer:

Phone Number:

Email:

Signer's Signature:

Thumb Print:

Service Performed:

- ☐ Oath
- ☐ Acknowledgment
- ☐ Jurat
- ☐ Other:

Identification:

- ☐ I.D Card
- ☐ Credible Witness
- ☐ Drivers License
- ☐ Known Personally
- ☐ Passport
- ☐ Other:

I.D. Number:

Issued By:

Issued Date:

Expiration Date:

Document Type:

Date/Time Notarized: **AM** **PM**

Document Date:

Fee Charged:

Printed Name and Address of Witness:

1.

2.

Witness' Signature:

1.

2.

Comments :

Record Number:

NOTARY RECORD

Printed Name and Address of Signer:

Phone Number:

Email:

Signer's Signature:

Thumb Print:

Service Performed:

- ☐ Oath
- ☐ Acknowledgment
- ☐ Jurat
- ☐ Other:

Identification:

- ☐ I.D Card
- ☐ Credible Witness
- ☐ Drivers License
- ☐ Known Personally
- ☐ Passport
- ☐ Other:

I.D. Number:

Issued By:

Issued Date:

Expiration Date:

Document Type:

Date/Time Notarized: **AM** **PM**

Document Date:

Fee Charged:

Printed Name and Address of Witness:

1.

2.

Witness' Signature:

1.

2

Comments :

Record Number:

NOTARY RECORD

Printed Name and Address of Signer:	Phone Number:	Thumb Print:
	Email:	
	Signer's Signature:	

Service Performed:	Identification:		I.D. Number:	
☐ Oath	☐ I.D Card	☐ Credible Witness	Issued By:	
☐ Acknowledgment	☐ Drivers License	☐ Known Personally		
☐ Jurat	☐ Passport		Issued Date:	Expiration Date:
☐ Other:	☐ Other:			
Document Type:	Date/Time Notarized:	AM PM	Document Date:	Fee Charged:

Printed Name and Address of Witness:	Witness' Signature:
1.	1.
2.	2.

Comments :	Record Number:

NOTARY RECORD

Printed Name and Address of Signer:	Phone Number:	Thumb Print:
	Email:	
	Signer's Signature:	

Service Performed:	Identification:		I.D. Number:	
☐ Oath	☐ I.D Card	☐ Credible Witness	Issued By:	
☐ Acknowledgment	☐ Drivers License	☐ Known Personally		
☐ Jurat	☐ Passport		Issued Date:	Expiration Date:
☐ Other:	☐ Other:			
Document Type:	Date/Time Notarized:	AM PM	Document Date:	Fee Charged:

Printed Name and Address of Witness:	Witness' Signature:
1.	1.
2.	2

Comments :	Record Number:

NOTARY RECORD

Printed Name and Address of Signer:	**Phone Number:**	**Thumb Print:**
	Email:	
	Signer's Signature:	

Service Performed: ☐ Oath ☐ Acknowledgment ☐ Jurat ☐ Other:	**Identification:** ☐ I.D Card ☐ Credible Witness ☐ Drivers License ☐ Known Personally ☐ Passport ☐ Other:	**I.D. Number:**	
		Issued By:	
		Issued Date:	**Expiration Date:**
Document Type:	**Date/Time Notarized:** **AM** **PM**	**Document Date:**	**Fee Charged:**

Printed Name and Address of Witness: **1.** **2.**	**Witness' Signature:** **1.** **2.**
Comments :	**Record Number:**

NOTARY RECORD

Printed Name and Address of Signer:	**Phone Number:**	**Thumb Print:**
	Email:	
	Signer's Signature:	

Service Performed: ☐ Oath ☐ Acknowledgment ☐ Jurat ☐ Other:	**Identification:** ☐ I.D Card ☐ Credible Witness ☐ Drivers License ☐ Known Personally ☐ Passport ☐ Other:	**I.D. Number:**	
		Issued By:	
		Issued Date:	**Expiration Date:**
Document Type:	**Date/Time Notarized:** **AM** **PM**	**Document Date:**	**Fee Charged:**

Printed Name and Address of Witness: **1.** **2.**	**Witness' Signature:** **1.** **2**
Comments :	**Record Number:**

NOTARY RECORD

Printed Name and Address of Signer:	Phone Number:	Thumb Print:
	Email:	
	Signer's Signature:	

Service Performed:	Identification:		I.D. Number:	
☐ Oath	☐ I.D Card	☐ Credible Witness	Issued By:	
☐ Acknowledgment	☐ Drivers License	☐ Known Personally	Issued Date:	Expiration Date:
☐ Jurat	☐ Passport			
☐ Other:	☐ Other:			
Document Type:	Date/Time Notarized: AM PM		Document Date:	Fee Charged:

Printed Name and Address of Witness:	Witness' Signature:
1.	1.
2.	2.

Comments :	Record Number:

NOTARY RECORD

Printed Name and Address of Signer:	Phone Number:	Thumb Print:
	Email:	
	Signer's Signature:	

Service Performed:	Identification:		I.D. Number:	
☐ Oath	☐ I.D Card	☐ Credible Witness	Issued By:	
☐ Acknowledgment	☐ Drivers License	☐ Known Personally	Issued Date:	Expiration Date:
☐ Jurat	☐ Passport			
☐ Other:	☐ Other:			
Document Type:	Date/Time Notarized: AM PM		Document Date:	Fee Charged:

Printed Name and Address of Witness:	Witness' Signature:
1.	1.
2.	2

Comments :	Record Number:

NOTARY RECORD

Printed Name and Address of Signer:	Phone Number:	Thumb Print:
	Email:	
	Signer's Signature:	

Service Performed:	Identification:		I.D. Number:	
☐ Oath	☐ I.D Card	☐ Credible Witness	Issued By:	
☐ Acknowledgment	☐ Drivers License	☐ Known Personally		
☐ Jurat	☐ Passport		Issued Date:	Expiration Date:
☐ Other:	☐ Other:			
Document Type:	Date/Time Notarized: AM PM		Document Date:	Fee Charged:

Printed Name and Address of Witness:	Witness' Signature:
1.	1.
2.	2.

Comments :	Record Number:

NOTARY RECORD

Printed Name and Address of Signer:	Phone Number:	Thumb Print:
	Email:	
	Signer's Signature:	

Service Performed:	Identification:		I.D. Number:	
☐ Oath	☐ I.D Card	☐ Credible Witness	Issued By:	
☐ Acknowledgment	☐ Drivers License	☐ Known Personally		
☐ Jurat	☐ Passport		Issued Date:	Expiration Date:
☐ Other:	☐ Other:			
Document Type:	Date/Time Notarized: AM PM		Document Date:	Fee Charged:

Printed Name and Address of Witness:	Witness' Signature:
1.	1.
2.	2

Comments :	Record Number:

NOTARY RECORD

Printed Name and Address of Signer:	**Phone Number:** **Email:** **Signer's Signature:**	**Thumb Print:**

Service Performed: ☐ Oath ☐ Acknowledgment ☐ Jurat ☐ Other:	**Identification:** ☐ I.D Card ☐ Credible Witness ☐ Drivers License ☐ Known Personally ☐ Passport ☐ Other:	**I.D. Number:** **Issued By:** **Issued Date:** **Expiration Date:**
Document Type:	**Date/Time Notarized:** **AM PM**	**Document Date:** **Fee Charged:**

Printed Name and Address of Witness: **1.** **2.**	**Witness' Signature:** **1.** **2.**
Comments :	**Record Number:**

NOTARY RECORD

Printed Name and Address of Signer:	**Phone Number:** **Email:** **Signer's Signature:**	**Thumb Print:**

Service Performed: ☐ Oath ☐ Acknowledgment ☐ Jurat ☐ Other:	**Identification:** ☐ I.D Card ☐ Credible Witness ☐ Drivers License ☐ Known Personally ☐ Passport ☐ Other:	**I.D. Number:** **Issued By:** **Issued Date:** **Expiration Date:**
Document Type:	**Date/Time Notarized:** **AM PM**	**Document Date:** **Fee Charged:**

Printed Name and Address of Witness: **1.** **2.**	**Witness' Signature:** **1.** **2**
Comments :	**Record Number:**

NOTARY RECORD

Printed Name and Address of Signer:	Phone Number:	Thumb Print:
	Email:	
	Signer's Signature:	

Service Performed:	Identification:		I.D. Number:	
☐ Oath	☐ I.D Card	☐ Credible Witness	Issued By:	
☐ Acknowledgment	☐ Drivers License	☐ Known Personally		
☐ Jurat	☐ Passport		Issued Date:	Expiration Date:
☐ Other:	☐ Other:			

Document Type:	Date/Time Notarized: AM PM	Document Date:	Fee Charged:

Printed Name and Address of Witness:	Witness' Signature:
1.	1.
2.	2.

Comments :	Record Number:

NOTARY RECORD

Printed Name and Address of Signer:	Phone Number:	Thumb Print:
	Email:	
	Signer's Signature:	

Service Performed:	Identification:		I.D. Number:	
☐ Oath	☐ I.D Card	☐ Credible Witness	Issued By:	
☐ Acknowledgment	☐ Drivers License	☐ Known Personally		
☐ Jurat	☐ Passport		Issued Date:	Expiration Date:
☐ Other:	☐ Other:			

Document Type:	Date/Time Notarized: AM PM	Document Date:	Fee Charged:

Printed Name and Address of Witness:	Witness' Signature:
1.	1.
2.	2

Comments :	Record Number:

NOTARY RECORD

Printed Name and Address of Signer:	Phone Number:	Thumb Print:
	Email:	
	Signer's Signature:	

Service Performed:	Identification:		I.D. Number:	
☐ Oath	☐ I.D Card	☐ Credible Witness	Issued By:	
☐ Acknowledgment	☐ Drivers License	☐ Known Personally		
☐ Jurat	☐ Passport		Issued Date:	Expiration Date:
☐ Other:	☐ Other:			
Document Type:	Date/Time Notarized:	AM PM	Document Date:	Fee Charged:

Printed Name and Address of Witness:	Witness' Signature:
1.	1.
2.	2.

Comments :	Record Number:

NOTARY RECORD

Printed Name and Address of Signer:	Phone Number:	Thumb Print:
	Email:	
	Signer's Signature:	

Service Performed:	Identification:		I.D. Number:	
☐ Oath	☐ I.D Card	☐ Credible Witness	Issued By:	
☐ Acknowledgment	☐ Drivers License	☐ Known Personally		
☐ Jurat	☐ Passport		Issued Date:	Expiration Date:
☐ Other:	☐ Other:			
Document Type:	Date/Time Notarized:	AM PM	Document Date:	Fee Charged:

Printed Name and Address of Witness:	Witness' Signature:
1.	1.
2.	2

Comments :	Record Number:

NOTARY RECORD

Printed Name and Address of Signer:	Phone Number:	Thumb Print:
	Email:	
	Signer's Signature:	

Service Performed:	Identification:		I.D. Number:	
☐ Oath	☐ I.D Card	☐ Credible Witness		
☐ Acknowledgment	☐ Drivers License	☐ Known Personally	Issued By:	
☐ Jurat	☐ Passport			
☐ Other:	☐ Other:		Issued Date:	Expiration Date:
Document Type:	Date/Time Notarized: AM PM		Document Date:	Fee Charged:

Printed Name and Address of Witness:	Witness' Signature:
1.	1.
2.	2.

Comments :	Record Number:

NOTARY RECORD

Printed Name and Address of Signer:	Phone Number:	Thumb Print:
	Email:	
	Signer's Signature:	

Service Performed:	Identification:		I.D. Number:	
☐ Oath	☐ I.D Card	☐ Credible Witness		
☐ Acknowledgment	☐ Drivers License	☐ Known Personally	Issued By:	
☐ Jurat	☐ Passport			
☐ Other:	☐ Other:		Issued Date:	Expiration Date:
Document Type:	Date/Time Notarized: AM PM		Document Date:	Fee Charged:

Printed Name and Address of Witness:	Witness' Signature:
1.	1.
2.	2

Comments :	Record Number:

NOTARY RECORD

Printed Name and Address of Signer:	**Phone Number:** **Email:** **Signer's Signature:**	**Thumb Print:**

Service Performed: ☐ Oath ☐ Acknowledgment ☐ Jurat ☐ Other:	**Identification:** ☐ I.D Card ☐ Credible Witness ☐ Drivers License ☐ Known Personally ☐ Passport ☐ Other:	**I.D. Number:** **Issued By:** **Issued Date:**	**Expiration Date:**
Document Type:	**Date/Time Notarized:** AM PM	**Document Date:**	**Fee Charged:**

Printed Name and Address of Witness: **1.** **2.**	**Witness' Signature:** **1.** **2.**
Comments :	**Record Number:**

NOTARY RECORD

Printed Name and Address of Signer:	**Phone Number:** **Email:** **Signer's Signature:**	**Thumb Print:**

Service Performed: ☐ Oath ☐ Acknowledgment ☐ Jurat ☐ Other:	**Identification:** ☐ I.D Card ☐ Credible Witness ☐ Drivers License ☐ Known Personally ☐ Passport ☐ Other:	**I.D. Number:** **Issued By:** **Issued Date:**	**Expiration Date:**
Document Type:	**Date/Time Notarized:** AM PM	**Document Date:**	**Fee Charged:**

Printed Name and Address of Witness: **1.** **2.**	**Witness' Signature:** **1.** **2**
Comments :	**Record Number:**

NOTARY RECORD

Printed Name and Address of Signer:	Phone Number:	Thumb Print:
	Email:	
	Signer's Signature:	

Service Performed:	Identification:		I.D. Number:	
☐ Oath	☐ I.D Card	☐ Credible Witness		
☐ Acknowledgment	☐ Drivers License	☐ Known Personally	Issued By:	
☐ Jurat	☐ Passport			
☐ Other:	☐ Other:		Issued Date:	Expiration Date:
Document Type:	Date/Time Notarized: AM PM		Document Date:	Fee Charged:

Printed Name and Address of Witness:	Witness' Signature:
1.	1.
2.	2.

Comments :	Record Number:

NOTARY RECORD

Printed Name and Address of Signer:	Phone Number:	Thumb Print:
	Email:	
	Signer's Signature:	

Service Performed:	Identification:		I.D. Number:	
☐ Oath	☐ I.D Card	☐ Credible Witness		
☐ Acknowledgment	☐ Drivers License	☐ Known Personally	Issued By:	
☐ Jurat	☐ Passport			
☐ Other:	☐ Other:		Issued Date:	Expiration Date:
Document Type:	Date/Time Notarized: AM PM		Document Date:	Fee Charged:

Printed Name and Address of Witness:	Witness' Signature:
1.	1.
2.	2

Comments :	Record Number:

NOTARY RECORD

Printed Name and Address of Signer:	Phone Number:	Thumb Print:
	Email:	
	Signer's Signature:	

Service Performed:	Identification:		I.D. Number:	
☐ Oath	☐ I.D Card	☐ Credible Witness	Issued By:	
☐ Acknowledgment	☐ Drivers License	☐ Known Personally		
☐ Jurat	☐ Passport		Issued Date:	Expiration Date:
☐ Other:	☐ Other:			
Document Type:	Date/Time Notarized: AM PM		Document Date:	Fee Charged:

Printed Name and Address of Witness:	Witness' Signature:
1.	1.
2.	2.

Comments :	Record Number:

NOTARY RECORD

Printed Name and Address of Signer:	Phone Number:	Thumb Print:
	Email:	
	Signer's Signature:	

Service Performed:	Identification:		I.D. Number:	
☐ Oath	☐ I.D Card	☐ Credible Witness	Issued By:	
☐ Acknowledgment	☐ Drivers License	☐ Known Personally		
☐ Jurat	☐ Passport		Issued Date:	Expiration Date:
☐ Other:	☐ Other:			
Document Type:	Date/Time Notarized: AM PM		Document Date:	Fee Charged:

Printed Name and Address of Witness:	Witness' Signature:
1.	1.
2.	2

Comments :	Record Number:

NOTARY RECORD

Printed Name and Address of Signer:	Phone Number:	Thumb Print:
	Email:	
	Signer's Signature:	

Service Performed:	Identification:		I.D. Number:	
☐ Oath	☐ I.D Card	☐ Credible Witness	Issued By:	
☐ Acknowledgment	☐ Drivers License	☐ Known Personally		
☐ Jurat	☐ Passport		Issued Date:	Expiration Date:
☐ Other:	☐ Other:			
Document Type:	Date/Time Notarized:	AM PM	Document Date:	Fee Charged:

Printed Name and Address of Witness:	Witness' Signature:
1.	1.
2.	2.

Comments :	Record Number:

NOTARY RECORD

Printed Name and Address of Signer:	Phone Number:	Thumb Print:
	Email:	
	Signer's Signature:	

Service Performed:	Identification:		I.D. Number:	
☐ Oath	☐ I.D Card	☐ Credible Witness	Issued By:	
☐ Acknowledgment	☐ Drivers License	☐ Known Personally		
☐ Jurat	☐ Passport		Issued Date:	Expiration Date:
☐ Other:	☐ Other:			
Document Type:	Date/Time Notarized:	AM PM	Document Date:	Fee Charged:

Printed Name and Address of Witness:	Witness' Signature:
1.	1.
2.	2

Comments :	Record Number:

NOTARY RECORD

Printed Name and Address of Signer:	**Phone Number:**	**Thumb Print:**
	Email:	
	Signer's Signature:	

Service Performed: ☐ Oath ☐ Acknowledgment ☐ Jurat ☐ Other:	**Identification:** ☐ I.D Card ☐ Credible Witness ☐ Drivers License ☐ Known Personally ☐ Passport ☐ Other:	**I.D. Number:**	
		Issued By:	
		Issued Date:	**Expiration Date:**
Document Type:	**Date/Time Notarized:** AM PM	**Document Date:**	**Fee Charged:**

Printed Name and Address of Witness: **1.** **2.**	**Witness' Signature:** **1.** **2.**

Comments :	**Record Number:**

NOTARY RECORD

Printed Name and Address of Signer:	**Phone Number:**	**Thumb Print:**
	Email:	
	Signer's Signature:	

Service Performed: ☐ Oath ☐ Acknowledgment ☐ Jurat ☐ Other:	**Identification:** ☐ I.D Card ☐ Credible Witness ☐ Drivers License ☐ Known Personally ☐ Passport ☐ Other:	**I.D. Number:**	
		Issued By:	
		Issued Date:	**Expiration Date:**
Document Type:	**Date/Time Notarized:** AM PM	**Document Date:**	**Fee Charged:**

Printed Name and Address of Witness: **1.** **2.**	**Witness' Signature:** **1.** **2**

Comments :	**Record Number:**

NOTARY RECORD

Printed Name and Address of Signer:	Phone Number:	Thumb Print:
	Email:	
	Signer's Signature:	

Service Performed:	Identification:		I.D. Number:	
☐ Oath	☐ I.D Card	☐ Credible Witness		
☐ Acknowledgment	☐ Drivers License	☐ Known Personally	Issued By:	
☐ Jurat	☐ Passport			
☐ Other:	☐ Other:		Issued Date:	Expiration Date:
Document Type:	Date/Time Notarized:	AM PM	Document Date:	Fee Charged:

Printed Name and Address of Witness:	Witness' Signature:
1.	1.
2.	2.

Comments :	Record Number:

NOTARY RECORD

Printed Name and Address of Signer:	Phone Number:	Thumb Print:
	Email:	
	Signer's Signature:	

Service Performed:	Identification:		I.D. Number:	
☐ Oath	☐ I.D Card	☐ Credible Witness		
☐ Acknowledgment	☐ Drivers License	☐ Known Personally	Issued By:	
☐ Jurat	☐ Passport			
☐ Other:	☐ Other:		Issued Date:	Expiration Date:
Document Type:	Date/Time Notarized:	AM PM	Document Date:	Fee Charged:

Printed Name and Address of Witness:	Witness' Signature:
1.	1.
2.	2

Comments :	Record Number:

NOTARY RECORD

Printed Name and Address of Signer:

Phone Number:

Email:

Signer's Signature:

Thumb Print:

Service Performed:

☐ Oath
☐ Acknowledgment
☐ Jurat
☐ Other:

Identification:

☐ I.D Card
☐ Credible Witness
☐ Drivers License
☐ Known Personally
☐ Passport
☐ Other:

I.D. Number:

Issued By:

Issued Date:

Expiration Date:

Document Type:

Date/Time Notarized: AM PM

Document Date:

Fee Charged:

Printed Name and Address of Witness:

1.

2.

Witness' Signature:

1.

2.

Comments :

Record Number:

NOTARY RECORD

Printed Name and Address of Signer:

Phone Number:

Email:

Signer's Signature:

Thumb Print:

Service Performed:

☐ Oath
☐ Acknowledgment
☐ Jurat
☐ Other:

Identification:

☐ I.D Card
☐ Credible Witness
☐ Drivers License
☐ Known Personally
☐ Passport
☐ Other:

I.D. Number:

Issued By:

Issued Date:

Expiration Date:

Document Type:

Date/Time Notarized: AM PM

Document Date:

Fee Charged:

Printed Name and Address of Witness:

1.

2.

Witness' Signature:

1.

2

Comments :

Record Number:

NOTARY RECORD

Printed Name and Address of Signer:	**Phone Number:**	**Thumb Print:**
	Email:	
	Signer's Signature:	

Service Performed: ☐ Oath ☐ Acknowledgment ☐ Jurat ☐ Other:	**Identification:** ☐ I.D Card ☐ Credible Witness ☐ Drivers License ☐ Known Personally ☐ Passport ☐ Other:	**I.D. Number:**	
		Issued By:	
		Issued Date:	**Expiration Date:**
Document Type:	**Date/Time Notarized:** **AM** **PM**	**Document Date:**	**Fee Charged:**

Printed Name and Address of Witness: **1.** **2.**	**Witness' Signature:** **1.** **2.**
Comments :	**Record Number:**

NOTARY RECORD

Printed Name and Address of Signer:	**Phone Number:**	**Thumb Print:**
	Email:	
	Signer's Signature:	

Service Performed: ☐ Oath ☐ Acknowledgment ☐ Jurat ☐ Other:	**Identification:** ☐ I.D Card ☐ Credible Witness ☐ Drivers License ☐ Known Personally ☐ Passport ☐ Other:	**I.D. Number:**	
		Issued By:	
		Issued Date:	**Expiration Date:**
Document Type:	**Date/Time Notarized:** **AM** **PM**	**Document Date:**	**Fee Charged:**

Printed Name and Address of Witness: **1.** **2.**	**Witness' Signature:** **1.** **2**
Comments :	**Record Number:**

*****If you have found this journal, please return to address located in the front of this book.*****

Made in United States
Troutdale, OR
11/03/2026

56844673R00113